Steelchest, Nail in the Boot and The Barking Dog

Steelchest,
Nail in the Boot
and The Barking Dog

The Belfast shipyard
a story of the people told by the people

collected and edited by
David Hammond

with photographs by Bill Kirk

Flying Fox Films
Belfast

Directors David Hammond Bernie Morrison Catherine Hammond Maurice Cassidy

Frontispiece: Fitting a propellor shaft to the 'Titanic'.

First published in 1986 by
Flying Fox Films Ltd.
37 Queen Street, Belfast BT1 6EA.

Jacket and book designed by Ralph Dobson
Printed in Northern Ireland by The Universities Press Ltd.

British Library Cataloguing in Publication Data

Steelchest, nail in the boot and the
barking dog: the Belfast shipyard: a
story of the people told by the people.
1. Shipbuilding — Northern Ireland
— Belfast — Employees — History — 20th
century. 2. Belfast (Northern Ireland —
Social life and customs.
I. Hammond, David, *1928-*   II. Flying Fox Films.
941.6′ 7082′ 0922   HD8039.S5G7.

ISBN 1 870044 00 2.

Contents

Foreword

People have been building ships for hundreds of years on the banks of the Lagan. The first ship that is recorded 'built in Belfast' set sail in September, 1636, for North America. She was the "Eagle's Wing", a vessel of 150 tons, and she carried a number of dissenting clergymen from a Belfast religious squabble.

Old paintings and engravings show a series of small boatyards, along the river Lagan, at the foot of the Cave Hill. But startling changes were made to that scene in the middle of the 1800s when two strangers, Edward Harland and Gustav Wolff, possessed of dynamic energy and flair, started the yard that has made Belfast famous for ships the world over. That was well over a century ago, long enough ago for tradition and customs to grow up.

It's among the workers there that you'd begin to look for such tradition and custom. They're the descendants of the fresh-faced countrymen who walked down to the Lagan to find work, away back in 1860. They came down from the Holywood Hills, from the shores of Belfast Lough, from Castlereagh — from the green townlands around Craigantlet, Comber, Moneyrea — small farmers, hedge carpenters, landless labourers, bringing little with them except the clothes on their backs, their strength and intelligence and leaving behind little more than the prospect of building "famine walls" for the landlord.

Heady Victorian zeal transformed them into riveters and riggers, joiners and shipwrights, building ships that became the most advanced vessels of their time, winning for their new home-city a reputation for innovation, integrity, excellence.

It was in the red-brick terraces of Ballymacarrett that they settled, under the iron gantries and towering cranes, near the roar of the foundry and the clang of the hammer, the surge and thunder of the engine works. There should have been what we now call *cultural shock*, a sense of loss, a pining for the rural ways. But they had moved in as families, as kinsmen, and their townland values survived and sustained them. They esteemed family life, the presence of the individual, the rhythms and the rituals of a close-knit community. Social planning or not, there was everything in Ballymacarrett that they needed — schools, churches, mission halls, shops, hospitals, clubs and pubs, houses with water taps and gas lighting, a playground in the streets.

It sounds idyllic and, of course, it wasn't for they had to live through depressions, wars, sectarian conflicts, the toil and the tryanny of the job. The men were careless of their safety and even their lives; they felt small, dwarfed by the tremendous scale of the ships, the forests of stagings. But they created men whose size and imagination matched the job — Big Aggie's Man, The Big Hallion, Steelchest — hard men to nick, men with ready tongues and a saying for everything. The shipyard, The Island, The Yard, became a territory where "boys do the work of men and men do the work of giants."

It seemed to them that the ships they built were the best ships in the world. The themes of this book however, are not about the ships but about the men who built them and the whole shipyard community of Ballymacarrett.

It was during the making of the film of the same name "Steelchest, Nail in the Boot and The Barking Dog", a period of some months, that I gathered the material, the hours and hours of speech, endless stories, anecodotes, jokes, that display the beliefs, rituals and customs making up the rich and disorderly pattern that is called folklore. In other words, the book is a story of the people told by the people, a self-portrait of a community, an *alternative history* that allows individuals to detail their own lives in a way that a conventional history seldom does.

To make this book I had to impose a structure on these long, friendly conversations. I found it necessary to interrupt the fluency of the chat, to put this story into one chapter, that story into another. Each chapter, in fact, is an anthology of stories with the same theme, and with its own conjunctions and collisions.

I interfered with the run of the speech as little as I could, punctuating it only to point up the original rhythms and trying to sustain its natural verve and energy, its characteristic Belfast tang. Some of it is repetitive, because the speaker required repetition to tell his own story, either to create suspense — as in the frequent use of "says he" — or to fulfil the rhythmic line.

There is very little complaining in the stories, little mention of the long hours, the hard work, the dirt, the harsh bosses. The bad conditions were there but there was always some way of retaliating, bucking the system, preserving your individuality in the heart of a vast workplace of cold metal and clamour.

For most of the people in the past there was an absence of choice, an inevitability about taking your place in the shipyard. Tommy Patton, who grew up 200 yards away, says "I always knew there was nothing else for me bar the shipyard." And Harry Fletcher says "You knew you had to come down here and you knew you had to make the best of it."

The way of life could not be changed for, as Alan Brew says, "You are building ships in the open, working against the elements ... you're not playing with bits and pieces of engineering. It's big stuff. And it needs to be handled with caution and experience." But, if it could not be changed, it could be compensated for, not by money for there was no big money to be earned, but by wit and humour, courage and, most of all, by an interest in the job and pride in doing it well, an awareness that you and your hardy kind were building ships "that would wear out the ocean."

David Hammond

Acknowledgments

I wish to express my appreciation to all those in the shipyard, Harland and Wolff's, who helped, first of all, in the making of the film and, then, in the preparation of this book.

I am also indebted to Victor Kelly for his knowledge and for providing introductions to key people in Ballymacarrett. Some of these were retired shipyardmen and all the more valuable — you can take the man out of the shipyard but you can't take the shipyard out of the man. Douglas Carson was equally helpful, particularly in the early stages of the research when an accurate historical basis was required. Of all those who supplied background information and guidance none was more enthusiastic and generous than Jim Patton and Bobbie Hanvey.

I got a warm welcome in the Welders' Club, also in Beechfield Primary School from Mr. J. Reddeck, and the children who featured in this book. Carol Bardon on our behalf spent a useful week there with the children, eliciting their own and their families' response to the shipyard community.

I received great help and encouragement early on in the project from Radio Telefís Éireann, Channel Four and the Northern Ireland Industrial Development Board.

The Northern Ireland Public Record Office and the Linenhall Library were, once again, ready to offer interest and information. So were the people of Blackstaff Press and David Brown in The Universities Press.

Ralph Dobson and Bill Kirk, in their respective roles of designer and photographer, were good company, and important contributors. Neil Johnston was a convivial and knowledgeable companion, likewise my old friend Sean O'Boyle..

My thanks, too, to Bernie Morrison, Catherine Hammond and Maurice Cassidy for their continuing belief in the enterprise. And, finally, my thanks to my wife Eileen for sharing in the work with enthusiasm.

Harry Fletcher

The happiest group of men you'd meet anywhere, the most rough-and-ready and hard-cut diamonds. Still the gentlest and meekest of people and you'd never get a more generous bunch of people. Their whole theme in life is that you come down here, and you've got to make the best of it. They certainly do make the best of it. You'd be afraid to take a day off in case you missed the antics that some of these fellows get up to. They are the most happy-go-lucky bunch of men that you would meet in any industry.

Chapter One

The Community

Harry Fletcher

William Drennan was an old uncle of my mother's and he drove hackney cars throughout the city of Belfast. And one of his contracts was with Harland and Wolff and he come down and drove the managers about, the top men, in the hack car.

"No matter what anyone says," he says, "the shipyard might be a hard place for some people to work in," he says, "but it's a good place, and there are good men down in the shipyard and you'll certainly learn a trade down there."

So that's the reason why I became a shipwright down in the yard. That old uncle had a long connection with the yard and he knew the chairman and all the top men, so it was easy enough for him to get us started, my brothers and my cousins and me.

Alec Delgaty

In my elementary school days, that was a right number of years ago, in the Thirties, my father was on the cross-channel boats that left from the Queen's Bridge there. I used to go on my holidays with him on the boat and I used to see round the engine room, used to do wee jobs around the boat. But then I got very interested in the shipping then, so really it led me into shipbuilding.

I started here at the age of fifteen as a boy helper first, working with the riveters. I heated rivets, and tossed them over to the holder-up, and he put them up and the riveter knocked them home, and that was my first job in the shipyard.

At that particular time they were on strict piece work, and it depended on the heater boy, whether they earned their money or not. They got so much per hundred rivets, so the more rivets a boy gave them the more money they earned. You had to be able to keep up a good supply of rivets, all just heated right.

I had about twelve shillings a week then and that was my wages. But on a Saturday morning, we worked Saturday mornings then, they used to give me half a crown each. A half a crown then was a lot of money, and that was five shillings extra, that was very nearly half of my pay then. On Saturday morning I was always sweating, you know, if they forgot to pay me whether they would give it to me on Monday or not. That was my introduction to the shipbuilding.

Herbie Atkinson

When I started in the shipyard in 1934 the welding was only starting. My father was a plater's helper and my brother was a painter. My grandfather was a blacksmith and all the cousins and uncles were blacksmiths. And it was a tradition that everybody followed from father to son. In those days you always had a fear, especially the apprentice welders.

We were on piece work then, we were earning good money, more than other apprentices. So we were heart scared of the other boys running and telling your father that you were earning more money than you were saying. You see, when I went in, it was seven and six a week and then we went on to piece work so we went from seven and six a week up to fifteen shillings and then a pound and even more. We were giving seven and six a week into the house and we were keeping the rest to ourselves. That was like gold then, seven and six. The apprentice welders were all going about smoking Gallagher's Blues and you name it. But we were all scared that somebody would tell that we were keeping all that money to ourselves.

Some of the boys gave in their full money but most of the boys kept the extra and put it into their pockets. You were always scared that you would get caught one day.

Another thing about the family connection was that there was always an eye kept on you. The boss could just go down and tell your father or your brother that you were misconducting yourself. They'd get you into trouble with your own family, they'd be at you for letting down the name.

Tom Boyd

Well, the street that I grew up in was Ulsterdale Street between Bloomfield Avenue and Ravenscroft Avenue. I wasn't born in it, in fact, I was born on the Woodstock Road but I lived the most of my life in Ulsterdale Street.

It was a great street for shipyardmen. The next door tenant he was a boilermaker on one side, the other was a plater, and there were fitters, riveters and shipwrights and people like that scattered about the street. It was dominated by the shipyard as far as employment was concerned and, of course, there were some people who worked in the ropeworks which was also quite convenient. That's the pattern that was common in Ballymacarrett in nearness to the shipyard. One could go out in the morning and easily walk in half an hour to your job.

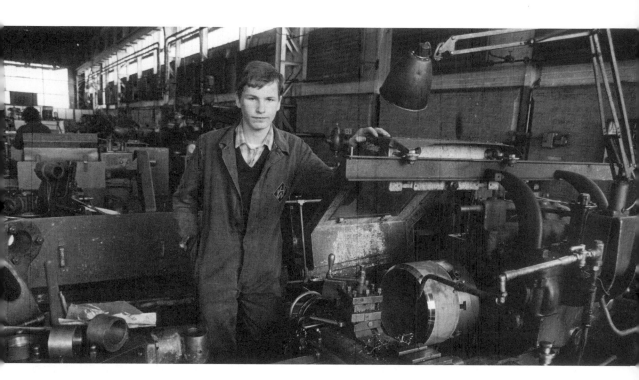

Peter Waddell

There's been four generations of our family with the shipyard up to now. There's me, my father, his father and his father before him.

I'm a fitter, an apprentice fitter. My father was a fitter, my grandfather was a machinist and my great-grandfather was a joiner. He worked on all the big liners.

16

Tom Boyd.

Tom Boyd

Mr. Nicholson was a north of Ireland man originally but he had gone to America and made a reputation out there as an evangelical preacher. There was a parade of shipyard men who left their work to go up and hear Nicholson in that church. They left the yard and marched up the Newtownards Road still in their dungarees.

I went to hear him once and I may say his style of preaching didn't appeal to me greatly. He was encouraging the men in the congregation to pay off their debts and so on.

He said, "If I had a magic wand that I could wave round this church, and command all this clothing that you have on you and haven't paid for, command it to rise off your body, to rise to the ceiling, I would have to shout, 'Brother Clark! Put out the lights!' Which wasn't very complimentary to his audience but it went down quite well, That was his style of preaching.

It is well-known that his converts took back the items that they had stolen out of the shipyard, paint, rolls of lino, wooden panelling, brass work, things like that, all were returned to the shelves in the yard. I don't know whether it was a measure of their repentance or not. But that actually did happen.

It's also true to say that we had troubled times in the Twenties between Protestants and Catholics and he did exert some influence to calm things down. That's to his credit.

Tommy Patton

Yes, I listened to Nicholson many a time at the Custom House steps. It used to be a great debating area round there. Oh, Nicholson put a terrible lot of people away, away to Purdysburn, so he did. He put the people mad, there was no doubt about it. You see, he had them away up in the air with religion, to be perfectly honest with you, a terrible lot of people took religion too seriously. It went to their heads altogether.

Tom Boyd

I served my time on the opposite side of the bench with a splendid craftsman called George Preston. He was a member of the Brethren and was very honourable and straight in his dealings with things. From my point of view, being a boy, he appeared to be rather straight-laced. But anything I learned of significance about the trade of pattern-making I learned from George Preston. He ran a Bible class every lunch time and his fellows gathered round him and had prayers and probably a reading from the Bible. He never invited me to join them but that suited me.

Tommy Patton

Of course, there was rogues too. I remember a man telling me he went to visit a fellow one time that was off sick. He went to his house and he had half the shipyard there between linoleum, the best of brass, wood panelling, doors, paint and bits of carpet. He says before he left he asked him what time she would be sailing.

The riveter he was different. All he would have taken home would be a big heavy hammer.

Billy Napier

What does the cross mean to you and me? First of all, let us suggest the cross would signify that we're wrong. Do you remember the time whenever we were in school and we done our exercises and whenever we opened up our exercise book we saw a big cross? That indicated we were wrong.

Let us always remember that we were the guilty ones. Christ was the innocent one. In Him there was no sin. But He took our place at Calvary. Romans, Chapter three, verse twenty-three declares. "We all have sinned and come short of the glory of God." But not only does the cross tell us that we're wrong, but it tells us that we were loved.

Alan Brew

You are recognised as a shipyard man, a bit gruff and possibly a bit rough on some occasions. But there's a broad strand of humour of a very cynical nature, running through it. Because we are working, you know, against the elements, a large number of us in the open, summer and winter. It's quite some job building a ship either on the slips or in that building dock, in very unpleasant weather conditions.

You need to be fairly strong about things, both in your ability to do the work and in your outlook to get the work done. You need to have a strong approach to life and to be able to make decisions and carry them through.

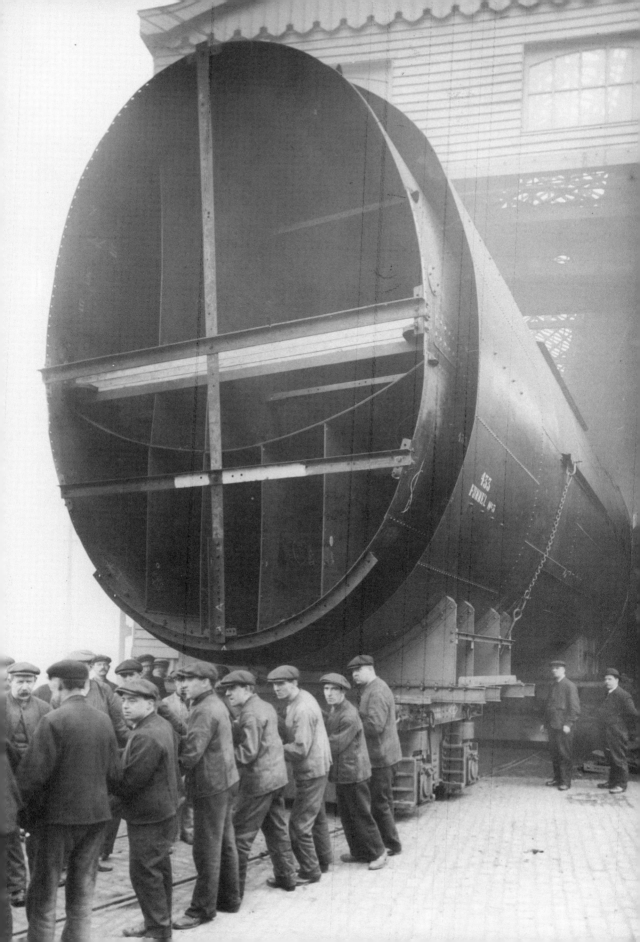

Harry Fletcher

I have always found that the Ulsterman is a very determined sort of person. And I found it very noticeable when I first came to work in the shipyard. Whenever I met the different types of people who were given the different tasks I found that their one theme in life was to do as good a job as it was humanly possible for them to do. They were dedicated men and they had one thing in common — they were shipyard workers. They took a pride in the job and they made sure that the shipyard came first, second and third in their lives. Their whole life and their family's life was built round the fact that they worked in the shipyard.

We have had all sorts of people down the Island — we've had sportsmen, we've had singers, dancers, comics, we've songwriters, we've book writers, play writers, all these particular types of people have worked in the shipyard here; and we've internationals, some of them is representing the country in different international games.

Jim Donaghy

You could always have told a shipyard man. If in the morning you went out without your piece there was no way that you would have starved for any one of the men there would have given part of their lunch to you.

Children of Beechfield Primary School with their murals of Ballymacarrett.

Harry Harwood

It was my Uncle Billy that painted the yellow on the cranes. They are called Samson and Goliath. Samson pulled down the temple and Goliath lost his head.

Thomas Thompson

My Granda painted the H & W on the big cranes. When he was away up there he could see the Isle of Man, he said, and the Mourne Mountains. He could look down into all the shops like wee toy ships. The men were like midgets.

One day he was in the cradle swinging from the top. The cradle was swaying back and forward in the wind. He was wearing a pair of yellow oilskin trousers for it was raining. A gust of wind blew up the leg of his trousers like a balloon. He was nearly blew off his feet but his mate saved him from falling.

Harry Fletcher

There used to be stories, too, about the riveters on piece work and they were true. There used to be a fence, you know, around Harland and Wolff's and the riveters used to climb the fence to get in at their work when the yard was closed on a Saturday or a Sunday. Every rivet they put in meant money to them, you know, and it took them to put in as many as possible in a day for to earn money. What they had to do was to prepare their job before they could put a rivet in and they got nothing for this preparation business, that was all part of their job.

So they woulda come over the wall on a Saturday or a Sunday and they woulda got their jobs squared up and got their bolts and washers ready. They'd even have screwed up part of the job so that they would have it ready to put rivets in on Monday morning.

There was counters in those days, too. They were the men who counted the rivets you put in and tested them and nobody liked them. They had few friends, they were like traffic wardens are today. But that's why you had always to be careful and you had to work as hard as you possibly could.

22

Alan Brew

In the engineering side we have had some high spots in building very large engines for not only our own yard, but for other shipyards. I have spent most of my life building large diesel engines, some of they very large indeed. We did, for instance, eighteen large diesel engines for a new shipyard, the Hyundai shipyard, when they were starting production of ships in Korea, and we delivered these at a rate of one a month. Which was quite a piece of export business and especially exporting engines to the Far East.

The approach to the work down here is fairly good-natured. A ship, you see, is a big and sometimes dangerous article. You need to have your wits about you when you're building a ship in the open. Similarly in the engineering side, building these very large diesel engines and running them, we're not playing with bits and pieces of engineering. It's big stuff and it needs to be handled with caution and experience. Everybody rubs along fairly well here. There are rows and disagreements, but we usually see the other fellow's point of view and try to keep the work going.

It's not as closely planned and organised as some other industries are. Maybe it can't be, maybe that's one of our weaknesses. But I know there's a great deal of scope for individual activity and achievement here, that should attract the younger men of that outlook and it does.

Ships have different personalities, of course. You really don't know what goes into a ship. But one ship, for instance, certainly can produce an excellent performance, without you really knowing really how she's achieved it. And in some other ships not just quite as good. But, oh yes, ships are quite different, and have personalities of their own. How that arises, I have never understood and I don't think anyone else does.

Alec McAvoy

There's a few stories that when you get a few plumbers together and they have a pint in the bar the fingers are dipped into the pints and they are drawing out pipes on the bar of how they used to get out of a hole. There's many's a story told about how to get out of tricky situation in a bar with a pint drawn on the bar.

You remember the old bars. They used to have all these snugs and the little boxes. They all had their own particular box, maybe six or seven of them in there drinking pints, and the stories were flying then about the different things that happened. It was very true, they worked very hard and they did earn their money.

Tommy Patton

On a Friday night they were all heading up to the pub. The barman would have the pints of stout all lined up for them and then all he had to do was to top them up and hand them out. They would lose no time when the men came in.

The men used to knock off at half-past five and you would have seen them coming. If you were standing at Dee Street you couldn't

have got across the street for men walking. They were just walking down in droves and you couldn't have got across.

The men came from the Shankill and Sandy Row, and there is also fellows from the Falls. But the majority came from East Belfast, from Ballymacarrett.

There was a quare crowd of country fellows. You'd have wondered how they put up with the travelling and all that. The countryman, he was an early riser and the tale was going round that he was always bringing in fresh eggs and country butter so that the foreman would keep him on.

Harry Fletcher   Even while they are socialising, out, say, having a drink in a pub or even at a dance or anything like that, you always find that the shipyard has to come up in their conversation. They are always bumming about how good their trade is and about this particular ship that they are building, and about this particular oil rig that they worked on. There is great rivalry. The shipyard is in their blood, as they'll tell you. It never stops to amaze people, you know, whenever they are listening to shipyard workers telling stories.

John Gibb   At Memel Street was the **Ulsterville,**
At the corner of Short Strand on the Mountpottinger Road **The Standard Bar,**

And then over across the road at the corner of Mountpottinger Road at the Bridge End was **The Old Swan Inn.**

Just around the corner at least twenty years was **The Carpathia.**

Round the corner again there was a landmark, **Molly Keenan's.**

And next to that was **The Britannic** but it was called **The Brit.**

It was a good bar, a mixed bar.

The next would have been Templemore Avenue **The Waterworks.**

The next one was **The Eastern.** That one was at Dee Street.

Now starting from the other side of the road from Full's Arch was **The Electric Bar,**

Then later on **The Talk of the Town** was there.

The next bar to that was **The Gateway Bar** and round the corner was **The City Lights.**

The next was **O'Kane's** then, on the corner, **McKeague's Bar** and if you went in there you got a big wine for sixpence. But if you had plenty of money they would have charged you a shilling. That bought you the bottle of stout and you got the wine for nothing, that's the way it was. We used to say that when they gave you a big wine they gave you a brush with it. When you drunk the big wine you collapsed and you got up, you brushed yourself down and walked out. It was a blowey-up shop

And then the next bar to that was **The White Star,** that was at Kenilworth Street.

The next bar to that was at Gertrude Street, **The Old Judge** and the next one to that was **McMahon's,** that was at Josephine Street.

The next one to that was at Scotch Row, **Hastings' Bar,** we just called it **Scotch Row.**

The next one to that would be **The Belvoir Bar** and then **The Vulcan.**

Next at Welland Street **The First and Last.**

I am living there now and the next one is **The Bloomfield** and after that **The Clock.**

John Gibb.

Mrs. Tommy Patton He started work in the shipyard at fourteen and finished up as Lord Mayor of Belfast.

26

Tommy Patton

Och, the pawn shop was a real feature of life. As far as the shipyard men were concerned, it was a great feature of life. Because what actually happened was his best suit would have went in on Monday morning. Then when he got paid on Friday night he would have rushed up and got his best suit out. Then he would have worn it at the weekend and then on Monday morning it was back in the pawn again. Some of them were regular customers of the pawns in those days and this was the way it went, the suit in and out, in and out.

Alec Delgaty

Years ago, people used to think it was a good job down here — that the men didn't have to work. You see, at one time there was so many men here, twenty-one or twenty-two thousand men working in the ship building, it was hard to keep track of everyone, and some people got away with slipping away, slipping home. It was hard to keep track of everyone. Today it is a much smaller yard and you can tell where your men are at any particular time now, so nobody slips off now.

Sinclair Gowdy

Well, I lived in a street, a very famous street, Carnalea Street off York Street. This street had one famous son, James Galway, the flutist. James and his brother George and his father were all music-ally inclined, they all played music. James' father often did without his drink and his cigarettes, so as James could have a flute, a new flute.

Well, I knew the father extra well for he worked in the shipyard with me here. He was a straightener, what we called a straightener. He straightened out bumps in the shell plates and he was a charac-ter. He was always full of fun and the men called him Jimbo, Jimbo Galway. And it was nothing unusual walking home with Jimbo in the evening, and Jimbo would have threw his cap down on the ground with the crowd passing and started singing. People would put money in the cap and he would lift it and laugh at them and run off and put the money in the first charity box he come across. That was the father, he was always doing this type of thing.

Oh, he was like the rest of us, he had a tin bath and a kettle of hot water for washing and that was about the limit. We all did that in the kitchen houses. James, the son, wrote in his book about the father taking a bath in front of the fire and a few of the neighbours looked in to see him, and — it's perfectly true — he got up out of the bath and down the street after them. He was naked as the day he was born and he just laughed at them and went back in again. He did it for divilment. Galway's divilment.

James wrote in his book about the two pianos in the street. That was perfectly true because during the Blitz I remember as a boy them pulling the piano out of the houses in the height of the Blitz and somebody actually sat down and played it. I can remember it as if it was yesterday. And another lady she played the mandolin. We were quite a street for talent.

James himself wrote about me in his book and he said I wakened him in the morning singing going to work. Well, in those days I did sing. But there's nobody singing these days. They're not even whistling. That's something I notice nowadays. When we were younger everybody seemed to be whistling. You'd hear them up and down the street, men going off to work, milkmen, postmen, newspaper boys, whistling. You'd be lying in bed listening to them. But nowadays I don't know what's wrong with the people but I never hear them whistling at all.

It's hard to put a word on it. We have money now. But I often think of those days. We didn't have much money but we had comradeship. I suppose that's what we had.

John Gibb

I was coming out one day at quitting time and I was going to make over for the Frazer Street Bridge. I was coming out of the engine works and I seen about five chaps. I know two of them and their boss was standing with them.

I says to the boss, "Excuse me, sir. Could you tell me where Frazer Street Bridge is?" And he put his arm round me and started to direct me how to get through the engine works and round this and that. He says, "You will then see a bridge and that is Frazer Street Bridge."

I walked away and Sam McKay was telling me afterwards that he had to walk around the leg of the big crane for he couldn't keep from laughing. He says, "For God's sake, John, you were *born* in Frazer Street." The boss never even knew.

28

Alan Brew

Well, I suppose one of my first conscious memories is being brought down here in a tram, I think probably on a Saturday in the nineteen twenties, to see a passenger ship being built to finishing stage and being totally astonished with the size of the whole ship and all that was in it, the magnificence of its fittings. My association with the company runs from then. My father came here from England about nineteen ten or thereabouts, married my mother, who was a tracer in Harland and Wolff. My three brothers and I have all worked in Harland and Wolff for a good portion of our lives.

Now, my memory of the Thirties is, of course, a bit juvenile, but I can remember the effects of the Depression in the early Thirties. It was really triggered by discovering a memo in my father's effects after his death. It was from the cashier, telling him that his salary was being reduced from six hundred pounds a year to three hundred. There wasn't any discussion about it. It was just a statement of fact of what was going to happen. This had some bearing on our domestic affairs as I recall.

But fortunately it didn't last very long because there was a ship left Harland and Wolff at this time. I think she was called the 'Achimota', built for the Dempster Line. And when it was finished they didn't have any money to pay for it, so the ship lay for a while, and my father had the job of looking after the engines. After some time it was eventually bought back by an Australian company, and he was elected to go out to Australia with their crew. So, our fortunes looked up, because he then went on expenses and as well he had his three hundred pounds. He was away for, I suppose, a couple of years. Thirty three into thirty four, the worst of the Depression.

And then came a considerable revival in early shipbuilding with a very large order from the Castle Line for several passenger ships. That activity went on in an increasing pace right up to the start of the war, and as I got older, I got more familiar with the work and I was down quite often to see how ships were finished, and the significance of it all.

There was always a discussion in our house about what ship we were on and what was finishing. My father was known as an outside engineer, responsible for putting the machinery into ships and getting it running and then being responsible for its performance during the sea trials. So there was always a discussion at meal times. It was an unusual situation to have one's father either coming home at two o'clock in the afternoon from work or setting out at one o'clock to go to work, but that's the way things were done. He was on the shift system in those days and a lot of ships and engines were made very effectively and quickly.

Rightly or wrongly, all this family connection gave me an ambition to move in the direction of the shipyard and of course I did. I served my apprenticeship in the conventional way, then I went to sea with the Union Castle Line for six years or so and came back here as a junior manager in 1951, and I have been working in the Engine Works ever since. I've got now to be one of the old hands, as we call it, and I look back with pleasure on both my upbringing as a child of the industry and then being active in it for thirty-five years now.

Chapter Two

Down to the Yard

Alec McAvoy

The first day I remember starting with my father. I left school when I was fourteen years of age and I started as a message boy. I think the biggest surprise I got was boarding the tram that particular morning at Ardoyne and coming right down through the town. If you didn't get a Queen's Road tram you had to change in High Street. And the throngs that were in High Street! Both between Harland's workers and the aircraft! It was black!

I remember my father saying to me, "Grab you the hold of my arm till I get you on this tram" and they were actually hanging on the platform and the backs of the trams and everything, hundreds of men. And then the tram slowly made its way round the Queen's Bridge and the bicycles were there in thousands and all the people walking at that particular time in swarms. It was really amazing, everybody congregating, trying to get to work for eight o'clock.

And, then when you were put on board a ship for the first time, that was really frightening. When you weren't used to listening to riveters and caulkers all starting up with their hammers, you were really deafened and you were glad to get home at night. Your ears were ringing. It was a frightening experience to come practically straight out of school into a heavy industry like shipbuilding.

I often used to wonder — to go back to the story about the trams in High Street — why did the people from the aircraft queue in an orderly fashion and the people from the shipyard just mobbed the trams? There was always, you know a difference — aircraft workers, collar and tie, and shipyard workers, duncher and boilersuit. They were always that wee bit more — a rougher diamond. Let's just call them a rougher diamond.

Billy Morrison

Many a morning I was on the last leg myself to make the time office and the job was to jump on the tram — if you missed your step it didn't matter as long as you got your arm around somebody's neck. You held on there for grim death, because if you didn't get to the time office before the horn blew you lost out, you were booked out for the day. So it was very amusing to see the trams. They were hanging on in layers. Sure, you could hardly picture it now but there must have been a couple of hundred people clinging on to it. It was like bees round a jam pot.

32

Alec McAvoy

Harkness was the main man. All the carters used to come down to the yard and they all had whips and long leather aprons. When you were going home at night there was that many trams on the road, bumper to bumper. The tram lines were actually in the centre of the Queen's Road and each side of the Queen's Road was then clear for bicycles and carts. And there used to be as many men on the horse and carts going up the Queen's Road as was on the trams.

Then they had the old policeman who was at the top end of Station Street. I forget his name but he was very jolly. If there was ever a jolly policemen he was it. The volume of traffic he used to have to control was powerful and he stood there and he kept the whole thing going. You can imagine the tram cars, buses, bicycles, horse and carts and this great big sign at the head of the Queen's Road — DRIVER LET DOWN REINS GET OFF CART AND DO NOT OVERLOAD UP HILL. It was up there for ages.

| Frankie Flynn | There used to be a relief horse standing at the Queen's Bridge there, a trace horse, and when it seen the other one coming up with a big load it just went in front of your man and hooked on and then helped it up the hill. A big white horse. |

Harry Fletcher — There was one tram and Fiddler Moore was the conductor of the tram and he brought his fiddle with him every time he come down into the shipyard here. Well, he got to know most of the boys, if he didn't know them he would ask who they were. You'd a heard him coming down the road, and him fiddling away; and he would be making up a song about the fellows that he had on the tram and their carry-on outside Harland and Wolff's and even their carry-on inside Harland and Wolff's. He became one of the characters of the shipyard himself. You know, at times it was a pleasure to come to your work because you were nearly afraid to miss something by not coming.

Alec McAvoy — When you used to board a tram you could tell what people worked at during the day by just smelling. I was always able to tell the people that worked in the engine works because of the oil that they used on the lathes and that. There was that heavy burnt smell of

34

engine oil about them. The joiners, you could smell the wood off
them. And the shipwrights they used to caulk the deck and they
rolled like an oakum and they caulked this into the deck and you
could have smelled all the oakum off their hands. They used to sit
on the deck and they rolled it on their knee and you could have
smelled it off their trousers. Then you could have told the painters
by the linseed oil. The welders had a funny smell, too.

Billy Morrison

Then there used to be a ferry, too. Remember it? That was for the
York Street men and the men from down the line in Whiteabbey
and Carrick. It was the O'Preys and the O'Donnells that ran the
ferries.

Many a day just leaving the quay they'd be down to the gunwale
and there'd always be men at the last lap, flying down the quay
jumping on at the last minute. No matter how long you'd wait there
would always be some man left behind. You could watch him taking a running jump hoping he'd make the stern. He'd make an
awful sprachle to get on. But it wasn't the first time that a man
jumped off the quay, missed the boat and landed in the tide. We'd
all be cheering.

Chapter Three

Earlier days

Jim Donaghy

Well, my earliest recollections of the shipyard was when I first started I worked at a place called the Deep Water. And you worked from eight o'clock in the morning until half-past five at night and when you went aboard a ship that was red with rust, everything you touched was cold steel. You were put into a small tank and in that same tank you would maybe have had a man riveting, or maybe a squad of riveters, and you would have a caulker. So between the noise, the dust, the fumes, the atmosphere was really unbearable.

The steel was cold and even in the dead of winter there was no heating. In summer if you wanted a drink of water you had to go right off the ship down a gangway, under the jetty, where the only water tap was available. Conditions were very poor. Nowadays Harland and Wolff's workers is issued with industrial clothing, free footwear, showers to clean themselves up after a day's work and most of them go home in their good suits.

Harry Fletcher

The men in those days were very badly looked after, you had very little facilties. Take, for instance, what you saw when a ship was being launched. You found that what they done when a ship was being launched, they always put tallow and black soap, 'glowter', as they call it, on the slips. You would always have found the ship yard workers, all black trades expecially, after the launch, would be rushing over to the slips with their tins and boxes, and filling them up with this black 'glowter'.

That was the only means they had for washing, just a cold water tap maybe a bucket and putting her on a chaffer for her to heat the water up, that was the only means they had of washing themselves. Again, they had no facilities for putting away your dungarees. The ship yard workers went home in the clothes they worked in. Now we have the best of amenities. You could come in dressed as if you were going to an office.

Charlie Witherspoon

There was a plater called Lord Antrim. I don't know what his real name was, but he was the heart of corn, a kindly man, but a very coarse Christian, as we would say. And there was a story that one day he was walking down the Shankill Road with his wife. His wife was wheeling the pram and the pram was squeaking badly. He was a very impatient man but he stuck it for a good while. Then it annoyed him that much that he burst out, "For God's sake, Aggie! Throw the bloody thing over and put a drop of glowter on her!"

Charlie Witherspoon

When I started work in the shipyard as an apprentice there was a slump. It was in the nineteen thirties and there was no work to do. We were apprentices and they couldn't pay us off. But there was nothing to do, there was grass growing on the slipways.

So what we would do to pass the time was to buy a bottle of olive oil. Now, in those days you could get a bottle of olive oil for sixpence, and we used to spread one another with this stuff and lie and stew in the sun away down at the Deep Water.

But we sometimes got bored. There was a tug, I think it was called "The Hercules". They stole the lifeboat from it, and what we used to do, just at lunchtime, we would get into the boat, row across the river, tie it up about York Street, hide the oars, then run like hell around to the Hippodrome, which was a cinema at the time and where you could get in for three pence. There was always two big pictures, and at the end of the show we went out and ran like hell through the town all the way to York Street, got into our boat, rowed back across the river, and threw our boards in as we went out to prove that we had been there all day.

But sometimes instead of the Hippodrome there was a boxing booth across the road in York Street and we used to go over there and it was the tremendous sum of sixpence to get in and the boxers had some fantastic names. There was Machine Gun MacKenzie, Hard Hitting Christie and Buckets McGaughey. They called him Buckets McGaughey because nobody could knock him out. The only way you could knock him out, they would say, was to hit him with a ringside bucket.

Well, of course, the boxing booth episode and the Hippodrome episode was all in the firm's time. We were supposed to be in the shipyard all the time, but we weren't. But remember the fact that I was on fifteen shillings a week: we would not have grown very fat on that.

Alec McAvoy

When I started in the shipyard there was no place for you to change your clothes. There was no amenities like that. What happened when you got off the boat at night you used to have a trough with hot water in it and you went down there and you washed your hands. Now when you stop at night you can to into the amenities, bring your good suit in and go home like an insurance man. Nobody would know you worked in the shipyard. You just change your clothes.

Tom Boyd

When I was a child of about five or six years of age I remember being taken down to the shipyard by my grandfather on Sunday. There was a ship there that was being prepared but couldn't be launched during the week because of the high winds. The ship was called the 'Rotterdam'. They decided to try and launch it on a Sunday and my grandfather, who used to take me on walks round the harbour and the shipyard on a Sunday, he took me to see the launch. But the boat wouldn't move off the slips. Of course, the Lord's Day Observance Society said it was because they tried to launch it on a Sunday. But it was probably because they failed to put the slips in properly.

But I do remember looking at that big hull — they were launched stern first — and the bow projecting into the air seemed enormous to me. It's nearly eighty years ago but I can still see the red lead on the ship right down the whole length of the hull.

Then some years later, my father who was on the wages and time-keeping staff, he, together with other members of the staff, got tickets so that they could bring their families down on a Saturday afternoon to view the 'Olympic'. And my earliest memory is walking down the staircase, in what I suppose, one would call the saloon in the 'Olympic', and imagining that I was translated to a royal palace or something of that nature. It was so beautifully decorated; at least, it appeared so to me, young and all as I was — I was about eight or nine years of age.

I do remember in the Troubles during the Twenties, I was a boy, that there were scenes in the shipyard among the men. I can re-member Catholic men actually dived off ships into the Musgrave Channel to get away from the intimidation. We had a number of

Catholics working in the pattern shop. No one ever molested them there but they stayed away from work because they were afraid, not of anything happening to them in the actual pattern shop, but perhaps on their way to work. And even then as a boy I complained about this; it was utterly alien to my upbringing which was that you shouldn't insult anybody on the grounds of their religion. That's the way we were taught in our family, and that is retained with me. I would regard all denominations as equal. I'll not accept that any one of them is infallible; they all have their defects and their good points but at least they should be given equal consideration when it comes to matters of thought and liberty.

Joe Tomelty

I remember one day I forgot my piece and a man gave me a ham sandwich. It was a Friday.

"I'm not allowed to eat ham on a Friday," says I, "I'm a Mick".

So he says, "All right, Take the bloody ham out of it." So I took the ham out of it and I ate the bread. They were a decent crowd and I never heard any talk about my religion, never and I can tell you I'm telling you the truth. If you worked with a man, if he was a good mate he was a good mate. That was all about it. I was there for some years during the Forties and that was my experience.

Billy Morrison

I used to hear stories about the shipyard all right. There was a story, it must have been before the first World War, that a Sunday School excursion from a Protestant church in Belfast was stoned away up in Castledawson. And I think that there was trouble in the shipyard after than and Catholic men were driven out.

But I joined the shipyard in the nineteen forties and I never experienced any ugly behaviour towards Roman Catholics or any difference being made. There were several Roman Catholic men worked with me — Lou Doherty and his brother Tommy and Gerry McNeill. I knew Lou, of course, for years since were were boys in Whiteabbey. He was with me in the explosion on the 'Reina del Pacifico' and he died beside me in the Mater Hospital.

I remember a man hitting one of the Catholic men one day but that man was an arrogant waster, he'd have hit a clergyman never mind a Catholic.

When I was lying in the Mater Hospital for months after the explosion the Catholic men were always trying to get in to see me.

Tom Boyd

I first went down to the shipyard in the month of January 1917 to start as a messenger at the gatehouse. Then I was apprenticed to the pattern making and I started on June 19th, 1919. My apprenticeship was completed in 1924, and I worked as a journeyman for approximately a year and then a slump set in and I was out of work for almost two years. Then we were in again for a while and out again. I had a total of about six years' unemployment in the first ten years until 1934 — that's the decade from 1924 to '34. They started, of course, about that time to build naval vessels because there were signs of a war on the way. The war came all right. I continued in the yard until the Blitz of 1941 when the place was destroyed and we were scattered about Belfast, throughout various pattern shops. I went to Sirrocco works where I worked for a while.

Herbie Atkinson

Well, if you were out of a job, maybe you had been out for a lot of weeks or even months, you maybe heard that down at the shipyard there were starting men. So each different trade had to go down looking for a start to their particular place. When you went down there was always a crowd of men who had heard about these jobs too. You went maybe to the Main Yard, East Yard, Abercorn Yard or different places.

So in each of these places there was a crowd of men and that was called the Market. The platers had one Market and the helpers had their Market at a different place. There'd be a plater standing there and he'd want to start a helper, so he'd walk round and point to such and such a one and he'd say, "I want that one there." Well this chap he'd dander over, cap in hand, more or less, and go along with the plater and that was him started. It was the same with all the trades. The foreman would pick out the journeyman and the journeyman would pick out the helper. If you didn't get a start you just dispersed. There was maybe only three or four men started out of thirty or forty men.

So the rest of them just went home and waited until the following morning. This would go on morning after morning but there was always men left that never got started.

When we started in 1934, the East Yard was starting to open up, and in between the slips, it was all bog land, you know, soft ground. And it was full of staging holes filled with water. Many's the time you had to walk over to the temporary lights store, for to put your board in to get a light, and you had to return your light at night. And sometimes you were walking across there in the dark at five o'clock on a winter's night and you were falling into these pot holes, and you were full of muck up to your eyeballs. That was one of the hazards in the shipyard, in the East Yard at that time.

We had rats, we had mice, sometimes we even had dogs and cats, but we had a terrible lot of rats.

It was all according to where you left your piece down. Sometimes we locked it in a box, sometimes we put in into our coat pocket, but generally you had to be very careful where you left it. Because the rats was all over the boats. We used to, when we were in the double bottoms, we used to tie the bottoms of our trousers in case a rat would go up our legs. They were everywhere and they ate everything.

Then, of course, you had people like the caulkers. They were great people for going down into the tanks and getting rid of the rats when they were flooding the tanks to test them.

It was hell. Winter time was hell in the shipyard when I went in to it at first. You had rain, you had snow, you had no water gear, like you have now.

Jim Donaghy

At one particular time in Harland and Wolff — on the jetty at the side of a ship and even aboard ships at lunch times it would just have looked like Las Vegas in America with gambling. There was bookmakers, rubby-dub boards, anything you can name, by the hundred, pitch-and-toss, crown and anchor, poker schools.

John Gibb

Oh, aye, there was pitch-and-toss at the Deep Water where the toilets was. When you looked into the toilets all the doors had racing papers up and the bookies were writing dockets for horse racing and all the rest of it. That was at the Deep Water. There was a big toss, a very big toss. They came from everywhere, plumbers, coppersmiths, riveters, joiners, redleaders, riggers, painters, blacksmiths, pattern makers, labourers, foundry men, they were all there.

Alec McAvoy

Practically every lunch hour there used to be the pirate bookmakers and the rubby-dub men, as they called them, the crown and anchor game. They would have slipped aboard ship about five minutes before the meal hour and hung up the newspapers with the day's racing. The men would have went round the hangar deck of the aircraft carrier and wrote out their bet and give it to the bookmaker.

There used to be actually hundreds of men on board ship doing their bets and periodically the harbour police would have made a raid and there was a great scattering match for everybody to get off the boat. Of course, the bookmakers and the rubby-dub men had the boilersuit and the cap and nobody knew one from the other, so they always escaped. But it was more to keep it under control than anything else that they had the raids. Then on the jetties they used to run a pitch and toss in which many's a pound was won and many's a wage packet was lost.

44

Jim Donaghy

In my time there used to be a lot of sailors, what I called Asians. I don't know what religion these Asians were, perhaps they were Moslems or Hindu or Buddhist. When they used to sit and eat their rice at the meal hour a part of their religion was that, when they were eating you daren't cast a shadow over their food. This particular shipyard man one day walked past and cast a shadow over it and immediately everyone threw their bowl of rice over the side. So he thought it was a great joke every day at meal hour to walk by and cast a shadow! I think the poor guys ended up starving.

One of the luxury liners came in for repair, the SS 'Tusan', this Asian on the crew offered the shipyard men watches to buy, which he swore he had bought abroad. Everybody was coming from all parts of the shipyard to buy these watches at £5 a time and, at that particular time, it was the big white fiver note. The week the 'Tusan' sailed away they were raging. They discovered he had been buying the watches out of Joseph Kavanagh's in Smithfield in Belfast and selling them at double the price to the shipyard men. So we all had a good laugh at that.

Herbie Atkinson

If you walked to your work in the morning and it was raining, you would stay soaked for the rest of the day. Sometimes you would have tried to get dried out at the furnace, or the blacksmith's shop, or the heater boy's fire. But you had to go out and work if you wanted to get any money. Now if rain kept persisting, there was what you called 'the wet horn'. And when that wet horn blew, everybody had to go home whether you liked it or not. Your money stopped and you walked home again. There was trams but not everybody had tram money in those days.

Harry Fletcher

As I say, there were hard days, but again I think it has stood to the young men that did serve their time within the ship yard. Indeed, there is a number of them has went overseas and different places, and when they mention that they worked in Harland and Wolff's, most of the shipbuilders or any kind of industry is prepared to take then on.

Herbie Atkinson

When we were in the main yard the crane man got 'blood'. There was big squads in it, you see, and the crane men they ruled the roost as far as giving you a lift was concerned. So long as you were in a big squad you were O.K. But if you were on your own there, you had no chance of getting a lift. For the simple reason that you couldn't give any blood money. So the big squads they commandeered the crane because they had paid the crane man so much blood money. You had to wait till they were finished or take the load up the ladders on your back.

They were poorly paid, the crane men, you see, so they had to get a few extra shillings somewhere along the line. It was taken for granted, so it was.

When I started in 1934 there was no conditions at all, and it meant that if a young boy had to shift two hundred feet of cable, he had to carry it himself, roll it up, two hundred feet long. I couldn't tell you what weight it was, it would be maybe a hundredweight. But he had to climb, he actually had to take it up the ladder himself because he couldn't get a lift with the crane. He had to carry it up himself, you know. He was on piece work so he had to do it.

Charlie Witherspoon

Conditions were terrible for the men. You see, we were platers and if we got a load of angle irons in, we had to push them on buggies. It was very, very, very hard work and the buggies went on little tracks, like railway lines. You often splashed through deep puddles and of course, you got your feet and legs soaked for the day. There was an old joke in the shipyard that if you were pushing buggies you should expose your genitals — on the principle that if you worked like a horse you might as well look like a horse.

You have to remember that the yard was an island made up from slob land. They dredged the Lagan and dumped the stuff to make the island. It was all mud, there was no surface.

I remember being in the east yard and the wind howling in and the snow coming down in a blizzard and yet we had to keep on at our work and lift the steel plate because we were on piece work and if you didn't produce you didn't get any pay. It was as simple as that. And quite often we brought in angle irons from the racks with the frost thick on them. Your fingers were numb and then you lifted them on to the buggy, one by one, and they you pushed the buggy. But the terrible thing was when the circulation started to return to your hands and fingers. It was one of those things, you got used to it.

46

Charlie Witherspoon

You see, every ship had a double skin on the bottom. Well, when you were working in between those double skins there was a dreadful feeling, there was a dreadful feeling of being shut in, of claustrophobia, you know, as if you were in some ghost city. Especially if you were working at night, there was just the odd clang of a hammer, coming from far, far away and you felt absolutely isolated. I can't describe the claustrophobia or the sense of loneliness you felt when you were underneath the tank top.

There was always an element of danger. Now one simple thing that you would not do, you would not get your boots soled and get sparbles in them, because sparbles being steel, you know, were very slippy. You had to be careful, you would go on your neck.

Certainly it was dangerous but you got used to it. You were on the ground and maybe going up to the deck and you'd maybe half-a-hundred weight of angle iron on your back which meant that you were climbing a ladder with one hand and it was a long distance from the ground to the deck, maybe a hundred and twenty feet. You'd maybe climb up the first twenty-foot ladder and get on to the landing, climb up another twenty-foot ladder and maybe another ladder after that, and another three after that. So it was hazardous because you were climbing a ladder with one hand and the ladder was swaying and shaking all the time. Shipyard men thought nothing of it, but there were quite a few accidents.

But the most amusing story about an element of danger was told to me by my Uncle Billy. Now, at that time the shipyard started at six o'clock and you knocked off at eight o'clock for a half an hour for your breakfast. And it was during the first war, and platers were making plenty of money, loads of money, and this fellow came into work one morning absolutely drunk. He couldn't walk straight, he couldn't bite his finger. The men knew that he was drunk and he walked up the ladders on to the staging which was only three planks broad and he lay down on the staging and fell asleep. If he'd turned he'd be down to the bottom. They didn't know what the heck to do, and they daren't disturb him. So one man says, "I'll fix him." So he got a wee bag of six-inch nails and he went on to the staging and he hammered the six-inch nails through the man's coat and trousers so that he couldn't move. Then they got the crane down, they put the crane around the staging and lifted him safely on to the deck.

There weren't many jokes about pay, it was that low, but there were jokes about compensation, of course. A man would come in limping, and maybe the limping was justified after the first week of his accident; but after that he was as fit as a fiddle, it was maybe only a bruise. But he would still insist on limping, he would limp around the town hoping that people were watching him, expecially a solicitor, so that he could put in a claim for big compensation.

Tommy Patton

But you see there was no such thing as big compensation in those days. If a man got one thousand pounds he was very lucky and they counted on him to be set up for life. The men were always taking short cuts, taking risks to get the job done. The management didn't bother very much. If a man fell, he fell.

There was no strikes in those days because the boss used to say, "If you don't want the job there's ten men waiting at the gate there who'll take it."

You could never win a strike and the bosses would say, "Let them go and their bellies will bring them back." Strikes were no good.

Charlie Witherspoon

Well, one thing struck me in the nineteen twenties when I was serving my time here. There was no real liason between management and worker. It was them and us, and it stayed that way. The only manager who had any influence on the shipyard workers was Lord Pirrie. Now, he was away before my time but the old hands remembered him and they always talked about him. They seemed to respect him. The old hands calculated, that he knew the Christian names of around three thousand workers in the shipyard.

Pirrie came from Conlig, County Down and I think he was the first home-grown Ulsterman to become one of the shipyard directors. There was a joke about Wolff, Edward Harland and Pirrie the three directors of the shipyard. Apparently at a special occasion a lady asked Harland, "What does a director do?.

"Well," he says, "Wolff designs the ships, Pirrie sells them and I smoke the firm's cigars."

Solly Lipsitz

I know that in my years there in the Forties things were very cold and that's one reason why most men used to gravitate towards the blacksmith shop on a winter's morning so that they got heated at the furnaces. That's where we met John Craig, the blacksmith.

I remember him particularly. He was a great chap. He was a Linfield supporter, and on a Monday morning John would be talking about the Saturday's match at Linfield, and he was particularly fond of a player called Davy Cochrane, he used to call him Twinkle Toes.

I was in the metal testing department and I thought that the ships were wonderfully built and it was interesting to note the comparison, for example, whenever any of the American ships came in. There wasn't anything like the same workmanship involved. They very often came in with cracks, fundamental cracks in the structure of the ship, something which never happened to a Harland and Wolff ship at the time. They were really very, very well built.

Harry Fletcher

Well, when I first came here to serve my time as an apprentice, Harland and Wolff had twenty slipways in operation then, and on each of those slipways there was at least one ship being built. On some of the slipways there was two ships, such as small corvettes or frigates or even small trawlers, and it would have a labour force of somewhere in the region of between twenty-five and thirty thousand manual workers. And ever so far along they had jetties and there were ships at every jetty. We were building naval ships of every kind and fitting out destroyers, minesweepers, aircraft carriers. Then others were ships that had come in for repair. We had a lot of naval vessels coming out of Belfast at that particular time and a lot of convoy escorts coming into Belfast for dry docking and for running repairs. They wanted them out on the run again as quick as they possibly could. They escorted the ships in and out of Liverpool, in and out of Belfast, across the Atlantic, the Russian convoys and different parts.

They were coming up to the Normandy landing, the invasion of Europe; there was a lot of ships in here being made ready for that particular operation, aircraft carriers, there was tank landing craft, troop carriers, frigates, all sorts of naval vessels. Plus the transports that were getting loaded up with the different war materials and that, and I came along here as a very, very young boy from school and I had no idea what the shipyard was like.

John Gibb

I think it was 1914 at Easter. The German plane came over that day. Linfield was playing at the Oval and there was this reconaissance plane come over that day and they came back in force the same night and they just destroyed the Newtownards Road. They just went along and machine-gunned it. But they always said it was easy to get up the Queen's Island because it was straight up the Lough and that led them right into the yard. They done an awful lot

of damage. The Main Yard was the worst hit, I'd say. There was a big landmine came down there on a parachute. The men all thought it was a German pilot and they ran over, but it wasn't and it blew up.

An American boat came in in 1942. If I can remember correctly she was the 'Claremont'. She was a naval ship, but she had soldiers on her, American soldiers, and German prisoners-of-war. They were taking the prisoners-of-war to the L.M.S. Railway as it was known then. They must have been taking them out to the country to camps or something. There was boilermakers working with me and there was four of us standing watching. Well, this man Alfie was standing watching the prisoners-of-war over on the quay. Joe Hunter was a charge hand and Alfie was a charge hand too.

Alfie says, "There's a boyo there I took a prisoner of war in 1914, Joe."

And Big Joe Hunter says to him "For God's sake Alfie! How did that come? He's only about 18, that boy."

And Alfie says, "Well, if it wasn't him Joe, it was his da."

It was the way he said it that was very funny.

It was in that particular boat the "Claremont", that was the first time I ever tasted corned beef and cabbage, Yankee style, and it was lovely. They made tarts and gave them to you. They made about 16 different flavours and down in the stokehold there was a percolator and you made coffee any time you wanted. That's what I was doing, I was making coffee or tea for the workers, the men that was on the boat working for Harland and Wolff.

They were very fond, the Yanks, of getting Irish money and English money, you know Free State money as we called it. Well, I was getting that for them and doing everything for them. They gave me boxes of cigarettes and cigars and, it must have been Christmas, for I got a turkey off them, a thing you never heard tell of, and a box of chocolates and I mind bringing them home for the wee girls and they were very welcome. But they were good to work with, the Yanks, and they were very friendly people. They weren't allowed off the boat and I used to do all the messages for them, get them drink and things.

Billy Morrison

As you know during the early part of the war the British shipping suffered a terrible lot in the Atlantic on the convoys. It was the most important work in our department where I was, that's the ship repair department, when ships were coming in. Many of them suffered badly through damage from torpedoes and such like, It was always a rush job to get them out again.

It was a vital link between survival and defeat and we were always encouraged to keep going, keep going, keep going. Anything we could do to get the ship turned round and back to sea again. So we were kept very busy. It was a case very often, if you had the stamina, to work all night and then work all the next day until half-past eight or half-past nine that night. That was quite a long shift and it was work all the time.

One of the more notable ships was the 'Georgic' from the Cunard Line. She was bombed and burned, and sunk and beached, and everything happened to her; and yet they brought her in and put her ship shape and got her to sea again. That was one of the most remarkable jobs they had, I think in, the west ship repair yard during the war. It lasted about eighteen months the repair job did, and by the time it finished I was well used to it.

Jim Donaghy

During the war, owing to the blackout, when the shipyard men were travelling down the Queen's Road most of them used to take a short cut in round the dockside. There was no lights and it was pitch dark. My grandfather unfortunately walked into the tide and was drowned. It was four days before they discovered the body — as far as I'm aware, it was trapped under Kelly's coal boat. My father took me as a child to the morgue to identify my grandfather and it is not a very nice story. Parts of his fingers and all had been bitten off with either the rats or the fish and I was brought up on this particular story in our family, so I was.

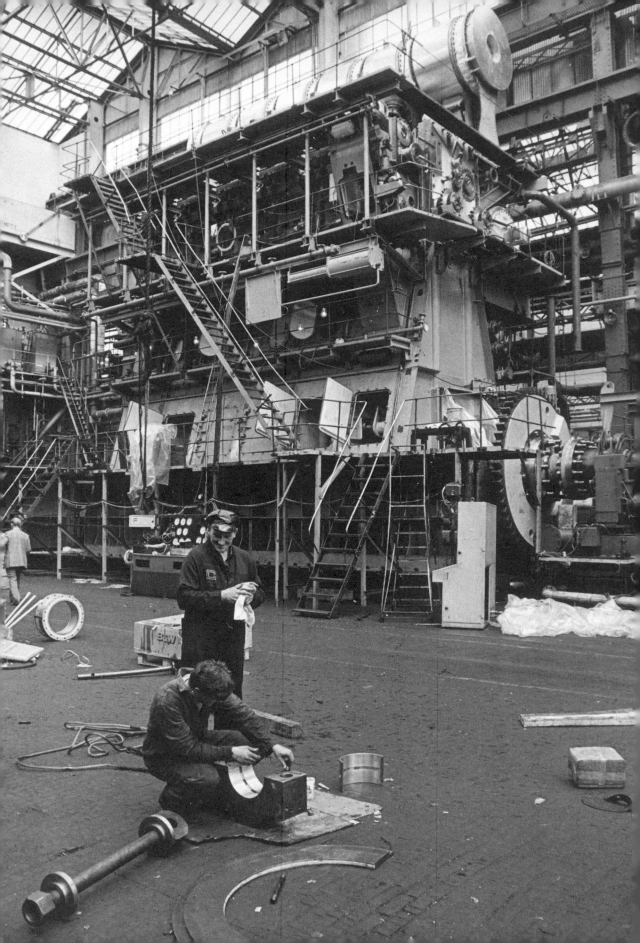

Chapter Four

Serving your time

Charlie Witherspoon

The first day I arrived at the shipyard it was terrible. I mean the men were all right, they treated me kindly. But the noises all around me — there was riveting and caulking and drilling and grinding and I don't know what. But remember at that time you didn't go in the first day and start to serve your time. At my trade, that was a plater, you weren't allowed to serve your time until you were eighteen.

Now I think one of the reasons for this was that there were heavy plates to handle: also you were climbing up gangways and up the stagings and it was dangerous. So they wanted you to have a bit of experience before they allowed you to start your time. But I remember that first day I stared all round me — I didn't know where the dickens I was. It was very puzzling. There were thousands of men, all going in different directions.

Bertie Waring

Well I started in Harland and Wolff serving an apprenticeship as a shipwright in 1952. In those days Harland and Wolff had a number of Ministry of Defence contracts. Mainly at that time there were four aircraft carriers and a number of frigates and minesweepers. The first job I was sent to was on an aircraft carrier.

I found in those days, that, if the journeyman you were sent to work with seen that you had an interest in what was taking place, then he was very anxious to pass on his knowledge to you. When I started I was earning something like one pound thirteen shillings a week. I worked in a large squad of shipwrights. In those days, being the apprentice in the squad, you were expected to do can-boy as well, make the tea, you know. And at the end of each week they came along and gave me half a crown each per week. So at the end of the week I ended up with two pounds a week can-money which was far more than I was being paid as an apprentice.

But in those days the journeymen had your welfare at heart as well. They didn't actually give you the two pound a week. They may have given you, say, ten shillings of that money and my mate saved the rest of the money until he accumulated say, ten or twelve or fifteen pounds. Then you would have to meet him in the town on a Saturday and he'd take you to Jameson and Green's and buy you some chisels and a hand hammer and a saw or a footadze.

And as well as that, when they seen that you were taking an interest they got some scrap material together and they showed you how to make a toolbox, how to do dovetailing, and how to make the drawer to fit in to put all the chisels and everything in. So I really looked forward to coming to work every day.

At that time I was a member of the Boy's Brigade and coming up towards the July holidays when we were off to camp in the Isle of Man or Southport, what they done was, they stopped buying me tools at a certain period and they saved the money up. And when it came to the July holidays they presented me with about twenty pounds. Now twenty pounds in those days was a lot of money. So I went home well pleased, I was checking my back pocket every few strides to make sure I wouldn't lose any.

Instructor John Harvey and two apprentices.

Harry Fletcher

It was a frightening experience to come down and see all those workmen working up on the stagings, and see all those ships. I had a fair idea and I'd seen some of the ships along the Donegall Quay but I'd never seen the size of some of the ships here and the men high up on the stagings.

The first day I went along with the journeyman he made it quite clear that I was here to serve my time and to learn my trade. That first journeyman that I worked along with happened to be a Roman Catholic. He told me that this was what his religion was and he says "That's different from you, but that is not to worry you," he says. "I'll make sure that you are going to turn out to be a good shipwright and I'll learn you all that I learned. It's a matter for yourself to take an interest." And he said that he had enjoyed his own time as an apprentice.

He says "In those days,"' he says, "they were men of iron," he says, "because they were very, very strict on you and they kept you at it from the horn went in the morning to the horn finished in the evening. You were there for to do your work and they saw to it that you done your work."

Reggie Gillespie   I remember the first day all right. My brother, he was already down the shipyard, he was a plater, an apprentice plater, and I was just out of school then, wanting a job. So he says, "Well then, we'll go down to the shipyard and get you started as a marker boy."

So away we went and I was on the bar of his bicycle, on a Monday morning going down to my first job. I'm as happy as Larry, going down for a job and all. So I'm whistling away there on the bar of the bike with my brother. And the next thing I felt my ribs being dug. He says to me, "You don't whistle going down to this place," he says," this is not a place you're happy to go down to."

But I didn't know that. That was my first job and I was glad to get something. That's why I was whistling.

Herbie Atkinson and Reggie Gillespie.

Alec Delgaty

I then went on to serve my time and started plating, steel working. At that particular time, we were building tanks. This is during the war years, you see, towards the end of the war, and the first ones when I came in here were Matilda tanks, and then we went on to Centurion tanks and Churchill tanks. I think these were for the desert warfare.

My job was putting the driver's seat in and the gunner's seat, for I was right and small and I was able to get in and bolt these down. That was really the start and then after three years at the steel working, I went to the welding and I've remained at it ever since.

I remember that I came in here one morning and started at eight o'clock straight from school. At ten past eight the foreman put me along with a squad of steel workers. I didn't know one man from another, I didn't know one foreman from another. At the present time we have a hundred and thirty working in this ship but at that particular time there was over a thousand. There was a big number of foremen too, and they all belonged to different trades, fitters, plumbers, you name it, they all had their own foreman.

There was no official teabreak in the mornings then, but you used to slip a cup of tea. You've heard about people boiling cans on the quiet at that particular time, so I was the look-out in case the boss landed.

The first day I was keeping dick they were drinking their tea and a foreman comes up the bay. I shouts, "Here's a foreman coming!".

They told me, "Don't take any notice of him. He's not our foreman,"

So go on ahead again, another foreman comes up the and I did the same thing, "There's a foreman coming!" and they all rushed back to work.

But they said, "That's not our foreman."

Another one came up, but I didn't bother them. It was their foreman this time and they all got caught on. So that was my first morning in Harland and Wolff's.

Harland and Wolff apprentices had a reputation all over the world for good workmanship. Many of them went to America and to Australia to England, Canada, New Zealand and did well, based on the skills that they had been taught in Harland and Wolff's. Oh, its reputation was very high.

Harry Fletcher

The footadze is one of those particular tools that whenever a journeyman come to teach you how to use it, he was always very particular to point out how dangerous a tool it could be. "A deadly weapon," as he used to say, "very lethal." You had to be very careful for it was always kept razor sharp. It was for reducing planks. As you know, there was a tremendous amount of wood used in those days on the ships. Most of the decks and all was wood, and down the hulls was covered in wood. It was important that you learned how to use the footadze properly. He always showed you how to sharpen them, and how to make sure that they were properly balanced.

There was some of the men who used the footadzes and they had them so sharp that you wouldn't a needed a plane when they were finished. The planks were just as smooth as if you had done them with a plane.

Harry Fletcher
honing the footadze.

I'll tell you about a funny custom they had when they were showing a young fellow how to use the footadze. They would put a wee line on the deck here and they would say, "Now, what you've got to try and do with this perfectly balanced adze, you've to try and hit that line."

So you were trying away, "Oh, you've got it! You've got it!" they'd say.

Once you done that a number of times they would have said to you, "You're getting it great. Just great. Now what you've got to do, is to do it blindfolded".

So you, of course, you were all on edge and you were willing to learn and you were going to show that you could do it just as good as anyone else. The next thing, someone would have come over and took your cap off-by the way they were putting it over your eyes. But it was someone else's cap, their own cap, maybe, they were putting over your eyes. They put your own cap down on the line and you are standing there blindfolded, with the footadze in your hands, ready. And you would hear, "Right now Harry, go ahead," and you started thumping away.

You'd hear, "You're doing well, Harry, great man, you're doing well, go ahead."

And then the next minute, "That's it!" They'd walk away and then you were left standing there blindfolded, by yourself.

You'd take off your blindfold. "Oh! Look at my good cap!" you'd say. Your cap was cut to ribbons with the footdadze. They'd all have been standing over there, roaring and laughing. So that was one of the tricks of the trade that you learned as far as the footadze was concerned. You mightn't have laughed because, after all, it was your cap. But then you saw the funny side of it. So it always come your turn and if you were that way inclined you could always get you own back on some other. Again it learned the boys to be careful and not just to take for granted things that people had told them.

Harry Lowry

Well, I could go back to nineteen forty six. I'm not originally a shipyard painter, I'm a towny, what they call a towny, and the job I was in I just decided to come down to the shipyard. And I'd no idea what was going on. So the first day I came down was a cold October morning. I started, got my pot and my paint and went out on to the ship and they put me on the catwalk of a tanker.

Now, I don't know whether you have any idea what the catwalk of a tanker is like, but the wind hits you in all directions, and I was so cold, believe you me, that after an hour, I regretted my move.

Joe Henry

I'm not a shipyard painter either, I served my time in the town. I came down here and it was about nineteen forty nine, I came down here, and I was working on an aircraft carrier, and I got lost four times it was such a large ship.

Jim Woods, Joe Henry and Harry Lowry.

Jim Woods

Well I started here in nineteen sixty five in September. Previous to that, I was a towny, too, I was working up the town. I worked along with my brother for a while and eventually I decided to come down and try the shipyard. I said to myself. "If I get Christmas out of this, I'll not be doing too bad." But I've been here ever since and I haven't regretted it. Many's a turkey it put on my table, and I managed to rear the family, and I've met some good chaps down here.

But you come down, and you're brought down by this gaffer, who takes you down below decks, and he shows you the job, and you get your pot and brush and up you get. It's altogether different from the town, where you're used to climbing up and down ladders and you ask the lady of the house what colour she wants for such and such a job. Down here they hand you a pot and a brush into your hand and the colours. "There's you, and there's it, go ahead."

Everything has a different name, the ceiling is the deckhead and the walls are the bulkheads, you've all sorts of names to learn for everything. Up in the town you were used painting ceilings and cornices and friezes and what have you.

Charlie Witherspoon

It takes my breath away now to think about it. We were only young fellows but it was a stupid thing, all the same. There were three kinds of birds that frequented the shipyard, they were gulls, starlings and pigeons. Now we used to catch the pigeons, and the way we did it was this.

We would take off our boots and socks and crawl along the beams of the cranes. That's well over a hundred feet above the ground. Now the pigeons used to roost in the hollow beams, and we used to crawl along on our hands and knees and stick a hand inside the lightening holes and grab a pigeon and then, of course, we wrung its neck, plucked it, and roasted it on a spit over a small fire. The pigeons were as tough as leather, but, of course, we thought we'd done something great and we said the pigeon tasted like pheasant.

Harry Fletcher

You've got the old timers, all the old seadogs, as we call the ship-wrights, and they always would have told you that the first ship-wright was actually Noah, for Noah used a footadze when he was building the Ark. So they classified Noah as the first shipwright. And that's why they are always very proud, because not only is the footadze still being used by shipwrights, but you'll find a great number of the ancient tribes used a type of footadze for digging out their canoes. So we're always very proud that our trade has been one of the first trades ever there was. We learned that when we were young fellows.

Most of the shipwrights in those old days would have always worn the dungarees. They had bib-and-brace dungarees and a dungaree jacket and a lot of them wore the deep-sea cap and some of them just wore the ordinary cap, the duncher, you know. Again, you would have got a lot of them with a collar and tie on and this made them a wee bit of a cut above everyone else. Another thing which they always prided themselves on was to try and keep themselves as clean and tidy as possible. They said a clean and tidy workman always leaves a clean and tidy job.

You always found that they had a small rag in their pocket to keep their hands and face clean. And this is what they always impressed upon the boys, too.

Again they were very, very strict. There was some hard taskmasters among them. They naturally would have asked the apprentices what they were doing at home and how they spent the evenings and they would have listened to the apprentices talking together, just to pick things up about their characters, to keep an eye on them.

There was a time journeymen would not allow apprentices to sit beside them. You see, when they would sit down at their meal hour, they's have kept the apprentices apart from sitting with the journeymen.

They'd have worked hard and kept the boys working hard. They were on piecework and the journeymen made more money than the apprentices, even though the boys worked just as hard. Some of the boys used to resent this but it paid dividends later on, so it did.

Bertie Waring On the morning I started in the shipyard, the shipwright that I was sent to work with told me, he says, "I suppose you've heard a lot of stories about the shipyard but I'll tell you one thing. You should be very careful when you're down here because they could steal the milk out of your tea."

I laughed at the time and thought that was a very far fetched story. So, when it came round to the meal hour, I was sent down to fill the tea cans and came up and handed my mate his can, I sat down and took my milk bottle out, emptied the milk into my tea. He says to me, "Bertie, reach us over your can a minute."

So I handed him over my can, and he lifted his can up and I noticed he had no milk in his tea. Then he poured half of my can into his can and then mixed them up, from one can to the other. Then he handed me mine back.

He says, "There you are. Didn't I tell you in this shipyard they could even steal the milk out of your tea?"

That was the first lesson I learned.

Charlie Witherspoon We used to play tricks on the gulls, we used to throw the remains, the crusts of our pieces. What we would do was, get two bits of bread and tie them together with a string about a yard and a half long and then throw them over the side. The gulls, of course, would pick them on the wing and it was great fun to watch to see two

62

gulls trying to eat the same pieces of bread simultaneously and then trying to pull them from each other.

And, of course, the apprentices played tricks on each other and sometimes the journeymen played tricks on the apprentices. You would maybe be working on the ship and the journeyman would have a little time to spare, and he would say to the apprentice, "Oh, we'll have to have a long stand for this. Now go you down to the store, and tell Joe you're my mate and ask him for a long stand. Tell him to hurry up for we haven't a lot of time to spare."

So the wee apprentice would run down the gangway and across to the store and say, "I'm Billy McKinstry's mate. He sent me over for a long stand."

"Aye, aye, all right. All right. Hold on."

And people would come for bags of bolts and bags of rivets and washers and all the time the wee apprentice was shifting from foot to foot growing more scared of being late back and at last he would say," Hey, what about my order? My mate sent me down here for a long stand."

"How long are you here?"

"I'm standing here over an hour".

"Well, I think you've got your long stand. So away back to your mate."

Another trick was that the apprentices used to engage a young fellow in earnest conversation and another apprentice with a brush and a tin of white paint would crawl along on his hands and knees up behind the gullible one and paint his heels white. Of course, this was an old shipyard joke and when the young fellow went out to go home the other workers would shout "Heel ball! Heel ball!" all the way up the road, in time with his walking and he would give everybody a bit of a laugh the whole way home. They would know he was just new.

Another trick they used to play, sometimes during the afternoon they'd get a piece of chain and chain your jacket hanging up on an iron peg.

Chapter Five

Nicknames

Charlie Witherspoon

We had a sort of First Aid depot in the main yard and it would have been about twelve feet square. It was all tiled and the man who ran it was called **Washing Soda.** He'd sell you packets of cigarettes and bars of chocolate just to make a few bob. But he was daft on washing soda. If you went in with a slight injury, he would have washed it down with washing soda and say, "Now, when you get home tonight wash it down with washing soda."

And the story was, that if a lead plate fell on you and amputated your leg he would have said, "Bathe it in washing soda." I never knew his name and I never heard him getting other than **Washing Soda.**

Frankie Flynn

There used to be a big fellow in the Copper Shop they called him **Wire Nail.** A big tall fellow, he wore a flat cap so he got a nickname **Wire Nail.** There was another man, a wee man, wee Norman, and they called him **Donald Duck** and they were walking up the Queen's Road one night and this other wee man, **Wee Harry,** the helper, he caught up on the other two and he says, "Would you mind if I walked up the road with you?"

Big **Wire Nail** says, "I'm blinking sure you're not. Do you want people to think there's a circus in town!"

Alec McAvoy

We had a foreman who was a boss fitter and he used to walk with the hands out slightly and the feet were spread. Of course, when he was walking about they used to call him **Stabiliser.**

Jim Donaghy

Nicknames was a very common thing in Harland and Wolff's. For example, you had one chap who worked with me was called **Steelchest,** another was called **Fowl Pest.** Then you had **Donkey Lugs** who was a plumber. This chap ended up a manager but he was commonly known all over the shipyard as **Buckets McGaughey.** And **Hard Wrought** was another one, **Tired Hands. The Barking Dog,** he was a famous character out the Newtownards Road, I didn't know the man personally but I always remember the name. There was **The Rajah.** Oh! **Takkerah** was another famous one all over the shipyard. Everyone knew **Takerrah.** When I started as a young man he was a middle-aged man but as I got older he got older. In fact he died just about a year ago, so he did.

Aye, **Nail In The Boot** was a plumber's helper. In fact, I knew the man well. As far as I know he is still alive. His name was Billy Coates.

STEELCHEST AND CO

66

I remember **Dread The Winter,** he had a bad pair of boots. I've heard of **Mountain Goat,** so I have.

John Harvey

Oh, stacks of nicknames. There was **Tear the Beef.** Then we used to have a leading hand and they called him **One Run Dick.** He wouldn't give you extra money when the job would have been wide. You'd need two runs, but he'd only pay you for one run. **One Run Dick.** Most of the welders had nicknames.

And then we had another foreman we called by the nickname of **Desperation Dick,** because he would come to you and say, "Leave that job and come to this one. I'm in desperation." He always said that and it was all over the ship, **Desperation Dick.** Then we had another fellow, we called him **The Mandarin.** He had a toe missing, and he walked along and kind of way put his foot out, and he had a wee moustache, and he had kind of sallow skin, so they called him **The Mandarin.** And then they also called him **Nail in the Boot** because he had a toe missing and him limping a wee bit.

Frankie Flynn

And then there was a fitter they used to call **Make and Break.** You know, he would have fitted a pipe and then he would have forgot he had no joint in it and he had to break it again and put his joint in. So he got a good name on himself, **Make and Break.**

Alec McAvoy

We had **Steelchest** in our department, an old chap called Geordie Hillen and Geordie was responsible for making all the lead tops aboard ship. **Steelchest** would have stood there day after day with that lead presser making the tops. It was a monotonous job to most people but Geordie took a great pride in it and dressed them all up and made a marvellous job and he just seemed to go on and on and

I think Geordie was actually seventy-seven years of age when he retired.

Frankie Flynn

Then the was an old fitter we had on the ship, Johnny Stranaghan from Lisburn, and he wrecked everything more than fixed it and they used to call him **Bits and Pieces.** I heard of another one called **Dread the Winter,** that was a fellow who had a hole in his shoe.

We had **The Squire,** he was a really old country plumber from Drumbo, Jimmy Ternaghan. **The Squire** was his nickname. Jimmy was always dressed with the plus fours and all and he was a great fellow for taking a hand out of somebody and he always had a wee Jack Russell with him. He goes into the bar this night with the wee chest-warmer pipe. He gets the pipe going, opens the tobacco tin, cuts a couple of leaves of tobacco and throws it on the floor and the wee dog jumps on it, snaffles it up and this chap in the bar says, "Are you not afraid of giving that dog worms?"

"Not at all," he says, "that wee dog loves a bit of tobacco."

But what nobody knew was that Jimmy, when he was getting his dinner he used to cut up a couple of slices of liver and put it into the box and that's what the dog got.

The same wee man he had a saying for everything. I used to collect the trade union dues and at lunch hour different people were in different areas and we used to go round and get the money. Jimmy was always in the plant and I headed out to the plant this day and Jimmy wasn't about and I jumped on the bicycle and was just coming back and I heard a shout from the far side of the road, Jimmy was waving the arms, you know, so I said, "It's all right, Jimmy. It will do me next week."

"Oh no," he says, "the man in the small boat must row close to the shore."

He wanted to pay weekly, he didn't want it to run for a couple of weeks. He had a saying for everything.

*Alec McAvoy
and Frankie Flynn.*

Harry Fletcher

There was a senior manager, in Harland's at that time, Mr. McCuaig, and his nickname was **Air Raid.** He was always trying to keep you at your work, a terrible man for trying to catch you out. It was war time so at the top of the Queen's Road there was a privately run canteen-cum-dining room, and a lot of ship yard workers used to slip up there in the morning to get a carry-out for their lunch. Some maybe who had not got up too early, they'd go up in there and have their breakfasts.

And the story is told that this particular day, with it being war time, quite a number of ships came from different countries all over the world, and there was a lot of Indian seamen, coloured seamen, in the canteen. And they were having a meal, and, of course, there was the usual number of shipyard men. But when the shipyard men were in they used to always leave a look-out outside to make sure there was no managers or foremen coming along. And here, this particular morning this look-out fellow ran in to the canteen and he shouted, "Air Raid!"

Well, all the shipyard men knew to get offside quick, to get out of the road but all the seamen, they dived in below the tables. They thought it was the Germans'

If any man was lame, or limping, he'd have been called **Nail in the Boot.**

Harry Fletcher

We'd men called all sorts of names here — **Bungalow** was a man who had plenty down here but nothing upstairs. An another man was called **Forty Watts** because he wasn't too bright.

There was a particular plater, and he was a big, hefty, strong lump of a man that would go through a brick wall. He was always just busting with energy and no matter what kind of job he did, no job was too heavy for him or too hard for him. He was just one of those rough and ready types. And he automatically got the nickname **The Big Hallion.** Well, there was a wee man sent along, who happened to be a riveter, another one of this particular type, who was always grabbing and pulling at this and that. He got the name of **The Wee Hallion.** Even the bosses referred to them as **The Big Hallion** and **The Wee Hallion.** Indeed some bosses asking for men would have said "Could you send me round **The Big Hallion** and **The Wee Hallion?**" Because they knew they would get a good job done.

Herbie Atkinson

Iodine Willie was in the main yard, and if you went in with your hand hanging off he'd give you nothing else only iodine. **Iodine Willie,** he had no facilities at all. One thing that was prone to happen, and that was getting steel in your eye. We stopped going to the First Aid because **Iodine Willie** couldn't see. You used to come out worse then you went in. He would have poked your eye out. It was the caulkers we went to instead. They always had needles for their work and they could have whipped a bit of steel out with no problem, you know. Anything only **Iodine Willie.**

70

Chapter Six

The Welders

John Harvey

Aye, it is a lonely job, welding, but to be a good welder you have to be honest. It's a personal satisfaction that you do the job right. That's the way I have always thought when I was welding — there'll be people on this ship and lives at risk, therefore it's up to me to do a proper job of welding.

It's very, very cold and in winter time the wind affects the welding, so you have to get wind protection. If the job's damp, you have to get a heater and heat the plates up for to dry up any condensation. If you didn't do that there you would get cracks in the welding. You wear extra clothes for the cold and then you have asbestos jackets and aprons and steel capped boots to wear. And you just have to try and keep warm as best you can. Some of them wear long underwear, you know, to keep them warm. Sometimes there, when you're working out on the staging there, high up on the staging, it's very, very cold. You would have to leave the job maybe and come down and find somewhere to get a bit of heat to get the circulation back again. Sometimes you're up maybe a couple of hundred feet high and maybe it's snowing.

It takes you to be experienced to do awkward positions there. You've got the direct overhead position which is a hard position and then you have obstructed work with things in your way, so that needs particular care.

They always say that there is no old welders, that no welders retire. They usually die. The welding is not a very healthy job and whenever you're welding you've got to have proper ventilation. To go into a place without ventilation you wouldn't live very long. But I think if you look after yourself and have good ventilation — I used to drink milk, a good lot of milk whenever I was young, and then I did a bit of cycling — that kept me kind of healthy. But I've lots of mates who have got, what you call, Welder's Lung. They've taken Welder's Lung and they're finished up for the rest of their lives. So it takes you to be very careful and have proper ventilation and look after yourself.

You think of things, too, while you are welding. You're watching your job all right but you also think, for it is a lonely job. You could be away down on a plate. You might go down there at eight in the morning and you mightn't see anyone till dinner time. Sometimes, the only way you know it's dinner time is when the power would start to rise, and you know then that people are starting to knock off for the meal hour. You wouldn't know what time it was, down in

the bowels of the ship. You would never meet anyone, you'd be on your own, you'd only see the arc of the weld.

Alec Delgaty

In my welding days, I went on the night shift. You see, I was on the night shift for seventeen years when I got married first. They laugh at that — just after I married I went on the night shift and stayed on for seventeen years. But it was extra money in the night shift, and you got away better with your work and it was piece work.

Welding is very lonely. You sit with this screen over your head and it takes about a minute, one point six minutes to burn an electrode. It you sit for one minute, a minute and a half, it's quite long. So you begin to wonder what way you are facing. Am I facing north? Or am I facing south? Sometimes, you have to wait till you're finished the electrode to see what way you are facing. It is a lonely job when you're doing repetition work.

I have welders in here who have travelled all over the world. During the Fifties there was a lot of them went to Australia and New Zealand, Canada. During the Sixties quite a lot of them came back. I have some men in here that chased money through the Middle East countries and Europe: Then they get to a certain age. Once they start to come into their fifties they come home to rest, and back in here again to settle down.

Herbie Atkinson

If you were welding on the deck in winter time you had snow and ice. You tried to clear that before you'd start to weld. In those days you used to carry black putty to try and make wee channels on the deck to keep the rain from running into your job. You'd do anything to get carrying on with your work to make a bit of money.

If you went down to the double bottoms at that time to weld, maybe you had to go up twenty spaces. You were on your own then. Nobody ever seemed to pay attention to it, but it was very dangerous. Certainly you were lonely. In fact, there was no one ever hurt in it.

But I remember an occasion when I was on the staff when I had to go into the double bottom for to count the welds. I was a rate fixer. I went up seven spaces and I came across a welder, and he had a temporary light on. When I spoke to him he didn't speak to me and I moved over to try to get into the space beside him. I seen his plug was still in his electric plug, but he still didn't speak to me. So I immediately pulled the plug out and it was like a balloon exploding, his breath. He was stuck to the deck, he was earthed to the deck. He just lay there till I got him out. He was O.K. but he had to go home and until this day he always says that I saved his life. That was the only time I ever came across an accident in the double bottom.

There was the smoke and the fumes and you had your own wee temporary light, but that was all. You had no fans at the beginning. You had no suction fans or nothing then, but gradually the welders become more organised. They started giving us fans, masks and everything else. But in 1934 to 1939 there were very few.

The blinks were an irritation of the eye, and they were the most

terrible thing ever you had. Sometimes they lasted around twenty-four hours. You got no pay. If you got the blinks, you didn't go into work, you sat in the house, your mother put cold tea on your eyes. You just had to wait until it went away. Water just kept running out of your eyes all the time — you could have went to the pictures, or to a dance, and in the middle of the dance, the blinks would have come on you, and you had to go home. It was like somebody throwing sand in you eyes.

You got the blinks through watching the arc of the weld with the naked eye.

Chapter Seven

'The Other Yard'

Reggie Gillespie

I got a job — it was flat bars I had to straighten, you see. They were six-inch flat bars, about three feet long. So we were at this machine that straightens them, I have a helper who works the wheel, which works a thing going in and out, called a ram. So I am putting in the flat bars — there was quite a few of these and I am wearing these gloves, they cover three fingers and a single finger and a thumb. So each time we were setting these flat bars in on top of a couple of angles, the helper just turns the wheel, brings the ram back and this went on for quite a while. Then one time I set the flat bar on the angle bar and all of a sudden the ram came through, caught my finger, whacked my finger off — the helper had forgot to pull the ram back. I looked at it and says I, "You've cut my finger off," and he almost fainted.

Anyway I walked round to the First Aid then and on my way I met a couple of blokes and they said, "What happened to you?"

I said, "I got my finger cut off," and I held up my hand and with the blood and the torn bits they nearly collapsed.

So round I goes to the nurse and she say, "Oh!", and gets all excited and takes me into the First Aid man.

He says, "We'll have to phone a taxi to take you to the hospital."

So off I went to the hospital. The finger was actually cut off at the bottom joint but they tapered it down and made it a bit neater. In fact I've known people for years and they haven't even known that I've lost a finger. It's a bit awkward now and again handling the one pound coins but that's all.

Well, I went to our solicitors, this was the platers' solicitors. They were in Waring Street, I think. The solicitor says, "You're the man who's lost the finger?" So we starts talking at that, and one thing led to another, and he starts talking me out of it, I felt.

He says, "How much money are your earning down there?" And I told him, and he says, "My goodness, there's a clerk over there and you're getting three pounds a week more than him. And you're going to claim off the firm!"

Says I, "I thought it was procedure, that you could claim for losing a finger." He started talking me out of all this, and it finished up all I got was £112. That was all I got for losing the finger.

Jim Donaghy

I can recall one time a bulk carrier sitting in the building dock. One day after the meal hour the men went back down into the duct keel to resume work and someone had left the oxy-acetelene burner on over the meal hour without turning it off, you know, at the taps. Well, two electricians, unfortunately for them, decided to light a cigarette and there was a massive explosion.

Most people were only on their way back to the boat, you know, first thing after lunch, and I was among the first people down into the duct keel, me and another chap who worked along with me, plus two strangers. It was all fumes and smoke and naturally all the lights was out in the duct keel. As you know, that is the bottom of the ship and we just had to more or less feel our way, tread our way, up the duct keel to try and find out was there anyone hurt or what had happened. Unfortunately, me plus the two strangers came across the two bodies of the two men who were both killed. Now I would reckon that was ten years ago.

Charlie Witherspoon When you see a big grey gull flying around you say, "That's not a seagull at all, that's an old shipyard worker, who has died and his soul comes back. He can't bear to be away from the yard."

Herbie Atkinson When you arrived in the morning you used to pick up your board and you went to your squad somebody might come up with the bad news that somebody had died. And instead of saying "He's dead", or "He's passed on", they'd say, "He's away to The Other Yard. There is no overtime up there, no setting sun, he'll miss that." Although they were very kind hearted, you know.

John Gibb

I had an accident one time. I was working on a boat that was all stripped and all. I was working on this skylight and I was putting bolts in. I was working on one plank, which wouldn't happen in the shipyard now. You would have about four planks. Anyway, I fell and my boss Bob Lewis was just coming in at the top edge of the room and lucky enough he caught me by the leg. I was hanging upside down and if I'd fallen I would never have spoken again. They carried me off over to the First Aid and they cut the trousers right off my leg, with the swelling.

I finished up in Dundonald Hospital getting about 109 stitches in my leg, but it was never right after it. I was told by one of the greatest men that was supposed to be in this country, Billy Ritchie, never to let them operate on it because all my sinews was twisted. I took varicose vains in the leg very severe and when summer came in I just couldn't walk with it nor nothing.

There was no legal aid or anything then. People was getting hands off and legs off and everything. I got a finger off in 1956, my whole wee finger and all I got was two and a half hundred pounds for it and the solicitor I had even threatened me.

Dickie Wallace

I was working up in the chain locker putting in sparring, it's a portable, wooden deck on top of the steel deck. The squad was a fellow called Cecil McCann, he's in Australia now, Geordie Lindsay, he's in Australia, too, and fellow called Tommy Speers, and a fellow called John Axon, and I just forget the name of the other lad, and myself. Och, we were all apprentices, although Cecil McCann, Geordie Lindsay and myself, were all senior boys.

We're up there and we're sparring the deck and the three youngest fellows they left us early for to go down the gangway. Well, then, it used to be that they kept you on the boat until, say, about three minutes to the blow. Cecil McCann, Geordie Lindsay and myself we were still working up in the forepeak stores.

Geordie Lindsay was the only one that had a watch, I think it was a Mickey Mouse one to tell you the truth, but he looked at it and he says to me, "Och, we've plenty of time," he says.

Dickie Wallace.

But it happened to be that the watch was five minutes slow and when we got to the deck for to get off the boat, the gangway had already broken. The three lads that worked with me, Tommy Speers and John Axon and the other lad, they were all on the gangway at the time and they went down with it.

I'm not an expert on these things. I can only tell you what I seen. The men were all held back on the gangway, you see, until the blow. There'd be a big crowd, too, on the deck waiting to get on to the gangway. They'd all be in a hurry to get off the boat and away home, they'd be pushing forward and the gangway would be getting more and more jammed. The ones on the bottom couldn't get off until they were let off.

It was a big high gangway, maybe seventy or eighty feet high with three or four landings. It was packed all the way down to the jetty. Even when it broke the men at the back of the crowd on the deck never knew and they still kept pushing forward.

Well, you can guess what happened to them when the gangway broke. They just fell, the ones that fell into the water were lucky. It was the ones that hit the jetty that didn't make it.

Tommy Speers, he was a weightlifter, och, a great big man. Well, after that accident, that was it. He got it all in the back, you know all the injury in the back. But he's doing well, now, for I keep in touch with him. He's in Canada but his sister she lives in our street and I ask her all the time about Tommy. He's doing well, thank the Lord.

I remember looking over the side of the boat that night, and the ambulances coming from the City Hospital and the Royal Victoria they just picked them up and took them away. There was nothing else you could do.

We couldn't get off the boat for ages. There was an awful crowd left on it. They had to cut holes in the side of the boat and put up new gangways for to take us off.

There was about twenty or thirty killed. I'm not the heaviest build of men and if I fell and a load of men fell on top of me it would have been curtains for me. It was the watch that saved my life.

John Harvey

There was a time when we were on piece work. This welder came over and said "What do you think you'd get for a cubic foot?"

Your man says, "I don't know. But put a big claim in. Put a big claim in anyway."

Herbie Atkinson

Harry Moffatt, he came from the Ravenhill Road, and him and I were right and pally because we would have walked up the road together to see our girl friends. At that time we were using a welding rod which had a very scenty smell off it and we were getting a terrible lot of burns. The elbow was the spot for burns. When you were holding the rod up, the sparks went down your sleeves and

landed in your elbow and this always got burnt first.

Well, Harry got a burn, and it turned to blood poison and he was out for three or four weeks. I met him one Saturday night at the Willowfield Picture House, and I asked him how he was doing.

"Not too bad," he says, "but I'm not starting work," he says, "I'm still blood poisoned."

The following Thursday he was dead. I went up to his house and I seen him and seen his people. They said he died of blood poisoning.

Well, I went into the shipyard the following morning and told the boys that Harry Moffatt had died and it was blood poisoning. A hour after that I was sent for by the boss, and he says, "I believe you were up at Harry Moffatt's house?"

I says, "That's right. I was up seeing his mother."

He says, "Well, do you know how he died?"

I says, "Yes, he died of blood poisoning."

"No. No. He didn't die of blood poisioning. Harry Moffatt would have been dead within a year. He had bad kidneys."

"Well, I'm only saying what I was told."

He says, "Never mention you that Harry Moffatt died of blood poisoning. He died through bad kidneys. Now remember that. He didn't die of blood poisoning through the welding."

And that was that. That was my warning. Two months after that, or maybe a month, appeared on the scene asbestos sleeves. They supplied us with asbestos sleeves for the welding to stop the burns.

He never got nothing. Harry Moffatt never got nothing and his family never got nothing.

84

James Donaldson, riveter.

Chapter Eight

The Riveters

Harry Fletcher

One particular time there used to be a row of black taxis at each end of the slipway on a Friday night. That was for all the riveters and heater boys because they were all on piece work and they used to work from the horn blew in the morning until the horn blew at dinner hour. Even during the meal hour the heater boy would have been away getting fresh coke for the fire and having it riddled and having all the rivets laid out.

At the end of the week they were paid as a squad and they were the big wages earners then — the riveters and the welders they went home in squads in the taxis and had a drink with their foreman.

Herbie Atkinson

Well, I thought that the riveters were the greatest buggers I had ever seen in my life. Real craftsman. The hand squad was slowly dying out when I went in in 1934.They were going into pneumatic. But if you seen them boys underneath the boat!

Now they had it to a fraction of an inch. A left-hander and a right-hander, a holder-up and a heater boy, bang, bang, all day. They never stopped. Unbelievable, great workers, craftsmen, no doubt. Nicest craftsmen I ever seen in a shipyard, and the hardest workers. They had to work, because they didn't get a penny piece until they pushed their first rivet in.

Tom Boyd

It is quite true there was a great pride in the workmanship of riveting. There was no welding in those days. If you had gone down to the shipyard in those days you would have seen thousands of men on the staging using hammers and hand riveting. There had to be a left-hand riveter and a right-hand riveter, if the left-hand man didn't turn up the right-hand man couldn't work because they were used to each other.

It took a squad of men to put in one single rivet. The heater-boy, the catch-boy and various labourers and what was called a holder-up besides the riveter. The holder-up held the heavy hammer against the inside of the rivet, he stood behind the plate so that it could solidly be hammered home. There was a great deal of pride.

Charlie Witherspoon

I was a plater and proud of the job but I always thought a lot of the hand riveting. Now here was this lump of a rivet coming through, with a holder-up at the back of it on the other side of the plate. But these two riveters on the outside would take these delicate hammers and they would hit the rivet through, bang, bang, turn about, hour after hour. They could put a polish on the rivet which was amazing. If there was any surplus left round the edges they took a little chisel and chipped it off and then hammered it up to a polish. That rivet was polished as if it was a walnut sideboard.

Tommy Patton

I started in the shipyard in 1928 and in those days there was no electricity, no lamps or anything like that. You had to get a great big paraffin lamp that showed you your way round the ships and when you couldn't get a paraffin lamp you got a red candle belonging to Harland and Wolff and you went all round the place with your red candle. That was your light in those days.

It was mostly hand riveting and the men in those days were very strong and powerful men. The very best of men and men who lived up to their reputation as great workmen. They were welcome no matter where they went in the United Kingdom, in any yard or in any firm.

I started work as a an apprentice riveter and there was four in the squad then. Two riveters, a holder-up and a heater boy. That's the man I started to work with first in the shipyard, Pepper McWilliam, and he lived in Hornby Street round there. They were wonderful men and you could have heard the rhythm of the hammers like a song. Because one minute their hammers were going fast and the next minute their hammers were going slow and there was a rhythm coming over that was a delight to listen to. Although it deafened you at times but it was a delight to listen to.

They had a language of their own because you have to bear in mind that there was sometimes a half inch plate between the riveters on the outside and the holder-up inside. You had to get some kind of information about what was going to happen next. So these men had a certain way of rapping a machine or rapping a hammer to tell the man inside what they wanted. As soon as he heard them rapping he knew what he was required to do. It was a language that only they knew. But if you were a riveter and you were walking along the road nearby you could have told what the squad was saying, what work they were doing.

I was born about two hundred yards from the shipyard. I was born and reared there. And I seen no other way that I could go bar go into the shipyard because my father worked there, I went in as a catch boy and that's the way I learned how the riveting was done. At that time in 1928 it was all hand riveting. The pneumatic riveting was created later. It was worked by air and there was a great noise off it and it took you to be a great strong man to hold the machine because a powerful force was required to knock in the big heavy rivets.

My imagination, no doubt, was very excitable about the shipyard because, as I said, I lived only two hundred yards from it. There I

Tommy Patton

could hear the rhythm of the riveting hammers and the voices of the working men. In the evening as it was beginning to get dusk, you could have heard this great noise coming over East Belfast and it used to be glorious to listen till it.

They were big strong men with big strong hands. They had a knack of dealing with everything. Even the new shaft — when the old one was done they had to get a new one. But when they got a new shaft they would sit down with a bit of glass, shaving away at the wood, shaving until they got a spring in the shaft. That helped the wrists and that helped the work.

And if a job had to be finished in a hurry they would have said, "Right. Throw the riveters in there. They'll get the job done". The riveters would let nothing stand in his road. He pushed everybody on. And not only that, but he would start and do their work as well as his own. He wanted to get the job ready so as to get the rivets in.

We never got great big money out of it. The riveters were called 'The Millionaires of the Shipyard' because they thought we were getting a considerable amount. But at the end of the day, for what you put, in you never got a terrible lot. You have got to look at it like this — I went in as a catch boy first and I got ten shillings a week. That's fifty pence now. And when I went to serve my time I got six and ninepence that was a reduction when I tried to become a tradesman.

I remember a boy called Steed who fell. He fell from the top of the stokehold right down to the keel and he got terrible injuries. They put a rivet bag over his face for they thought he was dead. But he survived and he came back to the shipyard. He was a wonderful man and he had a limp for the rest of his days.

Tommy Patton

It was very treacherous with the staging and stuff like that. You were carrying a bag of rivets, maybe a hundredweight, on your back, away up on the staging and the plank would be moving in waves. If you weren't cute enough to get the right wave it would throw you.

It's when when you went home to tell the wives the bad news that you found out the living conditions, if you understand me. There were no benefits, no welfare, the men were just depending on their work and if there was no work then they had nothing. The houses were wee industrial houses and they weren't great. The rent was about four shillings a week.

At the meal hour they'd be sitting down with their cans of tea and their piece and they would have been playing cards. Then the horn blew — it couldn't blow soon enough for the riveter, he was on the ball right off the reel. Then they'd push the other men to one side and get at their work. The noise would be serious and the other trademen, like the platers and the plumbers, would be shouting "Get that fellow knocked off! Get him knocked off!" and "It's terrible! You can't hear your ears!"

But you'd never have got him stopped. It was like trying to stop a train. But then as long as the manager heard the noise he knew the riveter was working.

The men were exploited, there was no doubt about that. They were making money but they were earning it, working long hours. They used to take 20% off all your wages for the riveting machine, the oil and the air, 20% went to Harland and Wolff.

Whatever you earned for yourself you had to make sure the heater boy got his money. I have seen men go home and pawn their suits to get the heater boy his money. Eighteen shillings, that's what they paid them in those days, the heater boy.

When you were riveting a ship you couldn't take a bit off it, nor you couldn't put a bit till it. If you had said to a man in the shipyard "Take a bit off that bulkhead" he would have went daft on you. You had a line and the ship must be brought to that line.

But when you're welding you can either burn a bit off or add a bit till it. Welding is the ruination of shipbuilding. I see ships getting launched on television these days and in my days at the riveting they'd never have been allowed out. You can see the ribs of the ship and great big indents in the shell.

In my opinion, out went the craft of shipbuilding when the welding came in. It was never a great trade, welding. I don't believe it would take you five years to learn it.

You take during the war — we had women welding, you know what I mean.

Jean Donaldson now Mrs. Jean Hunter.

Chapter Nine

A man and his daughter

Jean Hunter

My father was a very gentle man and he was a very kind man and very understanding. He gave me a lot of wisdom and he talked to me a lot and he was a very affectionate man too. He worked in the Belfast shipyard, Harland and Wolff. He always called it 'The Yard'.

It was lovely thing to look forward to my father coming home from his work. I'd have my school lessons done, no clock could tell what time he was coming in — but I knew he was coming. He always came in the back door, and the first thing he did was wash his hands and face. Then he came in and sat down in his chair and he got his cap and coat off and sometimes he managed to get his dungarees off and the tie loosened and the muffler off. But he used to fall asleep he was so tired. I was the only one who could make him waken up for his dinner. He was so tired. The work was that hard. His clothes used to be full of red lead and holes from the welding and he just looked very tired.

He had a very special piece which he loved and it didn't matter how often he got it during the week. It was Veda bread with loads of butter and crispy rashers of streaky bacon, cold. Sometimes he would come home at lunch time and not stay in the shipyard for his lunch and I would see him of course, being at the school across the road. So I shared it with him, and that was just like a feast to me, because of the taste of it and the smell of him and the taste of the bread and the bacon. It was different. It was really lovely, that is a beautiful memory that I have.

He just had a shipyard smell and I think that probably wives and children around my age would recognise it.

My mother used to have to make two pots of tea, one for her and me, which was semi-weak, and one for my father. He enjoyed shipyard tea which was about four or five spoonfuls in one pot and the gas turned on and brewed and brewed and brewed. They called it 'Let it stand' and it was so thick and so strong it seemed to keep the shipyard men going and I know they got it down the shipyard as well.

My earliest memory was my father carrying me down to the ship yard to see a launch. There were enormous crowds in those days, everybody turned out. I think they saw that the shipyard men got the day off. But everybody seemed to be there, men and women and children, families, all the dignatories. It was just a real day out, it was beautiful. The men who had worked on the ship were up on the deck, and maybe you would recognise one or two and they would be waving their caps and shouting and the cheers — I never heard cheers like it, never, never, before or since.

I remember my father coming home on one Friday night and he didn't wash his hands and face that night. He sat down and he started to cry. That's how sensitive he was. I fact, I had never seen a man cry before, I was around seventeen or eighteen, and he said "I got my cards".

He was just told, "Lift your cards on Friday night", and he walked out of the shipyard the same way he went in at the age of twelve. They were cutting down on welders and he had a big motor accident and he wasn't fully able to crawl along the pipes and do all the pernickety jobs that welders have to do. It did hurt him because he missed all his friends down there and all his pals and I think he missed the comradeship, too. He was sad for a long while.

My father had one very good friend in the shipyard and his name was Tossie Thompson and he came from the Newtownards Road. He played the accordion and I think he had a wee go on the banjo as well. He was very fond of music, any sort of music at all. I think it's his son that has to do with the Ballyclare Male Voice Choir.

There's one thing in particular that brings back those childhood memories. Its the smell of the shipyard, the red lead, the iron, the rust, the fumes, the oil, the wood shavings that comes from the shipyard and it comes home on my husband's clothes, because I married a shipyard man.

Chapter Ten

The "Seaquest"

Alan Brew

Well, I suppose the launch of the 'Seaquest' must have been one of the high spots. We were all wound up, the whole city was wound up about that. It was one of the few occasions where I noticed a lot of people coming down to see the launch, it really was an achievement for my shipyard colleagues to pull this off, doing what was said to be virtually impossible. And the 'Seaquest' itself was, of course, in its day, a very successful rig. It was a tripod structure built over three slips. The work was done in the Musgrave Yard.

I'm not a shipbuilder, I'm an engineer, so I can't speak for all the technicalities but it was a huge top heavy structure, which had to be built, then pushed down the slips and into the water. I think there was a serious risk of her turning over or falling sideways or doing something very dramatic. A variety of people had been saying, "It isn't on, you shouldn't do it," but it came off very successfully indeed. No one that was there will ever forget it.

Harry Fletcher

Another thing which they take a great pride in is the fact that they built the oil rig, the first oil rig built on slips. The Germans and the Japanese all these people said that we couldn't do it, even the Americans came off with it that we couldn't do it, and that we would never be able to get it into the water. Yet they launched that oil rig into the water, they finished that oil rig here, off three slips.

Jim Woods

Well the day that I remember most vividly since I came down to the shipyard was the day that they launched the 'Seaquest' round in the Musgrave Yard. It was a lovely day and there was thousands of people lined along the jetties along the Musgrave Channel Road. And the stage was set really for this thing just to go careering down the three slips and break in to several pieces. In fact this is what the Japanese and the Germans and all expected to happen and they were all there waiting on this taking place.

But, anyway, we were all wound up and, first of all, the "Seaquest" started to move imperceptively — you know you could hardly have seen it, just an inch at a time. The tugs they were all waiting, lying off the shore to get hold of her as she was launched. She started to move and they the crowd seen her coming down and there was a huge cheer went up.

Harry Lowry

I think half the shipyard was either laughing or crying that day. It was a terrific day and I'll never forget it anyway. It made me very proud.

Chapter Eleven

The 'Reina del Pacifico'

Alan Brew

There was one incident that had quite an impression on me when I was a young man in my twenties. One has to go back into a bit of history. The 'Reina del Pacifico' was a large passenger ship, built here in Belfast, I think she was put into service in 1931, one of the fastest ships in the world, with a most unusual engine, quite modern for the day, and she ran very successfully on the South American run for many years. She came back here after the war, for a total refit and alteration, back to passenger carrying from troop carrying. Eventually they had a sea trial which ended up in quite a serious explosion from the machinery, and quite a serious loss of life.

As it happened, I had just got home from sea, a day or two beforehand and was invited out on her by my father to increase my knowledge of engineering. But I refused, for being a young man, I had a lot of other interests of a more domestic and personal nature to look after when I was on leave. I'm quite grateful that I didn't go on the sea trials but, even so, it left quite an impact upon me and my subsequent career.

My father was in charge of this unusual engine, a quadruple screw installation, four twelve-cylinder diesel engines driving this ship along. Without going into too much detail, there was a fault in one of them, an explosion occurred in one engine and it caused a carry-on effect in the other three engines. So there was one very large explosion in the engine room, and my father, and, I think twenty-six other people were killed. It had quite an impact on the whole of Belfast at the time. This was, I think in nineteen forty-nine or forty-seven.

They'd been away several days up the Clyde and so on. I was sitting at home, we lived in Glastonbury Avenue at that time, at about half-past nine or ten o'clock on a Thursday night, wet it was too, I'd been listening to the BBC and I flicked the dial round to Radio Eireann, as it was called then, or Athlone possibly. I just caught the last sentence of the newsman at ten o'clock saying that there had been an accident on a large ship in the Irish Sea with loss of life. Well, I thought it could only have been the one ship so I lifted the phone to a senior colleague of my father's and said. "Have your heard?"

"Oh yes," he says, "I don't know what's happened but I'm just about to go down. Would you like to come?" And I said yes I would.

"Well," he said, "meet me at the BCDR and I'll take you in." So I got down there and this gentleman, Mr. Wilkie, brought me into the yard and we spent the night there. We were talking on the radio to the ship and they, of course, were very guarded in what they were saying. In a sense they didn't really know the extent of the damage and the injuries and deaths at the time. It was still a bit chaotic on board as the ship was towed in from somewhere well off the Cope-lands. We heard on the radio that my father was one of the injured.

It was, I suppose, about three or four o'clock the following morning that the harbour tug, a big tug that the Belfast Harbour Board had had built here, arrived in with the most seriously injured on board. So we went round to the Victoria Wharf to meet the 'Duchess of Abercorn', that was the name of the tug. They were taking all the injured to the hospital. Naturally I thought that I was going to meet my father.

But instead of that he was dead and his body was on board the tug. Eventually I had to go and identify the body and that wasn't pleasant.

The problem then was what to do about my mother at home. It's not the nicest thng for a young man at that stage to have to go home and tell the news at seven o'clock in the morning. One grew up very quickly with that.

Billy Morrison

One of the main tragedies in my part of the ship yard was the 'Reina del Pacifico'. Now she was originally a passenger liner, a lovely looking big ship. she weighed over twenty thousand tons and she had been used during the war years as a troop ship, going through a conversion to suit the troops. So, after the war, she had been brought to Harland's to bring her back to the passenger liner again. That was quite a job and quite an overhaul.

Following a major overhaul of that nature sea trials are always carried out. It could be three or four days up the North Channel or up to the Clyde.

Well, it so happened that we had been out on sea trials with the 'Reina del Pacifico'. We had done the compass run between Bangor and Black Head. Then we proceeded to the Clyde and at the entrance to the Clyde is the Isle of Aran and between the island and the mainland is the measured mile.

The measured mile takes a wee bit of preparation because the engines have all to be tuned up. You must set the fuel properly, test the compression and all that. You always do the measured mile twice, first with the flow of the tide, then a run against the flow of the tide. That gives you an average of how the ship is behaving. Strange to say, the owners of the ship are always concerned about the fuel consumption so the engineers have to set things to bring it down to the satisfaction of the owners, see that they are getting good value for their money.

All went well with the sea trials. We left the Clyde and we were heading home at cruising speed, around eighteen knots or that, only two hours out of Belfast Lough.

All of a sudden it was reported to me that this particular engine was showing heat. I had just completed a round of inspection around the four propelling engines and I was surprised when I got the report.

But I made my way to the engine room and many a time I think of the men who were standing there at the door — Mr. Brew, the Senior Manager and Mr. McKibben, his assistant and the fitter of the watch, Jimmy Collins. We were all more or less surprised that the heat should be showing on that door. Because, remember that we had been out for three days and through all the trials. But there certainly was a lot of heat inside that door.

There was no good guessing so I asked Jimmy for the spanners, to get the door off for inspection. But Jimmy hadn't even time to answer me. The explosion happened then.

The door came off in a half moon. The last nuts to give way were the two at the top and the bottom. The centre part was blown out and inside this half-moon was like an atomic bomb. It was just a big bulb of white heat.

I knew I was burned and I made my way away from the door but I didn't go very far, I couldn't go very far. I think I must have walked over to the ship's side and passed out. I remember then that I was being lifted, I'd a rope tied around me and I could hear the voices saying, "Watch his head. Watch his head."

But then I was only coming to for a few seconds and then passing out again. We were all put in the harbour tugs and we landed in the hospitals in Belfast. I ended up in the Mater. It all happened at about half four in the evening and I think it was five o'clock in the morning before we got to the hospital. Whoever had the job of dealing with us all on board ship I'd say had a terrible time of it.

I think I was saved because of where I was standing. There was only one door that did not blow off and that was the one behind me. Out of four engines and ten doors on each engine, that's forty doors, one door didn't blow off, and that's the one I was standing in front of. There were many people there that got fouled and injured badly by the doors and all the pieces of machinery all breaking and collapsing with this terrific explosion. All the steam and oil passed right through all four engines and did a terrible damage.

I couldn't have told you much about it, other than I could hear the people. Each time I came to for a few seconds I could hear the people yelling. I'm sure they were yelling with their pain. But I was gifted that day that I was unconscious. I wasn't aware of it, I was pitying these people who were burned. I thought to myself that I was not burned at all.

But there was a man came to visit me later in the hospital. He got decorated for it. His name was Geordie Crothers. He asked me where I went when the accident happened. I told him I just walked over against something perpendicular, that I could not go any further and that I just slid down and passed out.

"You know," he says, "you were the last man to be taken out. We thought we had everybody out of that engine room but I thought I'd go back and take a last look and I found you sitting beside a wee ladder". He reckoned that I could have been there anything from half an hour to an hour after the accident. I'd been sitting there burning or smouldering.

That's why I got burned so much from the neck up. You see all these eyelids burned, eyebrows burnt out, and my arms were all third degree burns. A strange thing is, that many doctors, my own included, have often said to me, "You know, boy, you shouldn't be alive, according to your burns."

They just can't explain it. So I could have been sitting for nearly an hour, because it took that time to get the engine room cleared and to get the ropes and haul all the injured out of it, and I'm still sitting there burning. Nobody had caught me on until Geordie came down for the last time.

There were only five of us who went to the Mater. You see they divided us out between the Royal, the City and the Mater. Well, I think, it was a small ward they put us into and there was five of us

— no, I beg your pardon, there was quite a number died, that's right. By the time I realised where I was, that could have been a lot of days after it, there was only three of us left in the ward, and then they had to keep us separate because there was always the danger of picking up a bug.

But, anyway, they treated us for the burns, for about a month, with the best equipment they had then. After the month's treatment we required skin grafting. Although in my condition they doubted very much if I would make it to Grimstead, because I was at my worst, they had to take a chance, because it was either go to Grimstead or go blind. The chance paid off and I started eating a wee bit.

During the time that we were in the Mater Hospital we got great attention. They couldn't do enough for us. There was one old Sister, I say old — she was aged — called Sister Regious. Well, I know that that women never left my bed. She tried to do her best, a wee bit of comfort, or even try to get me to eat a wee bit, I think the biggest job was to get me to eat something, because my mouth and all was burnt, everything was burnt. So you can guess what it was like to chew, to open your mouth. Every movement was agony.

Another case in the hospital was a man I knew well. He was called Lou Doherty. He was in my department, but I also knew him well from our young days in Whiteabbey. Well, it so happened that one day when he saw my sister visiting in the hospital he says, "That's Billy. He's in a bad way, poor fellow." He thought that my sister wouldn't know me.

You couldn't have made us out because our heads were like footballs with no features, we had no nose, no eyes, because the heads were so swollen. The head was just like a big blob there on the pillow. Poor Lou was saying that I was in a bad way, and yet when she came back the same evening again his bed was empty. She asked about him, and Lou had died. The shock was too much, and it killed him.

During my hospital time I was no respecter of persons. Of course, I was going through a terrible time and it was all the same whether it was the sister, or the nurses, or the doctors, ministers or anyone else. I never gave it a thought, I used to be yelling and shouting and giving off wholesale because of the torture of it. And then maybe I would pass out, I would just faint.

I couldn't give you all the gory details, the pain was terrific, the pain used to knock me out, just knock me unconscious. I don't know how long I'd be out, but by the time I came round again the dressing would be all done.

I would say that it remained with me in a kind of a way, that sometimes I'd be very straightforward. I might realise a little bit later on that I could have been a bit more diplomatic sometimes in my replies to certain people.

I was never embarrassed by my appearance, no, not in the least. I was in a bad way all right. My face was like a mask, it was hard and baked. I couldn't even smile or I couldn't even shape my mouth. But I was always a churchgoer and I thought nothing of just going up there and joining in the service as I normally would. I could have gone anywhere or met anyone.

A strange thing, I never felt like giving up because it never crossed my mind. It was the furthest thing from my mind. I never once thought about dying.

Sam McLaughlin, riveter on the Titanic, photographed in 1986 at the age of 97.

John Ned Quinn   I was coming with two buckets of water from the well down the orchard for the horses and this man was after coming out from Newry and he was coming up to the gate when I was coming out of the orchard.

And he says, "Jack," he says, "there's shocking bad news this morning."

I says, "What's wrong?"

He says, "This big ship," he says, "the 'Titanic' that sailed. She's to the bottom this morning."

Chapter Twelve

The 'Titanic'

Traditional

You faint hearted Christians, oh, listen to my tale
The gallant ship 'Titanic' for New York land did sail,
She was lovely, and the largest boat that ever yet was seen,
But she lies with fifteen hundred souls beneath the Atlantic Sea.

A beautiful April morning she steamed from Southampton Quay.
There were millionaires as well as poor bound for Amerikey,
There was joy and hope in every heart as she ploughed the ocean blue.
With a veteran Captain on her bridge, 900 men her crew.

All went well until that night in April it drew nigh,
'Twas in the middle of that night an iceberg floated by,
The 'Titanic' proudly moved along, unmindful of her foe,
When she got a crash, and awful smash, and cries from all below.

Brave Captain Smith was on the bridge and gave his orders clear,
His wireless operators sent his message far and near:
"Oh, save us, we are sinking fast," it was an awful cry.
Sad to relate, help came too late, fifteen hundred souls did die.

There was not much confusion, none thought the ship could fail,
The band was playing merrily, there was no storm or gale,
When suddenly the boats were launched, in rushed the waters wild,
The husband taken from his wife, the mother from the child.

The good old ship 'Carpathia' she heard the wireless cry,
And putting all her steam ahead, to the Titanic she did fly;
She saved all in the lifeboats, landed in New York Bay,
And all she left behind her now await the Judgement Day.

Tom Boyd

The shipyard was such an important feature of Belfast life with so many thousands working there, thirty thousand at that time. It was the chief thing featured on so many picture postcards — the huge gantries, and the huge cantilever cranes standing out against the skyline: It was a terrible shock to everyone, and even today it is still talked about. The memory will not go away.

106

Lord Pirrie.

Chapter Thirteen

Heroes and hard cases

Tom Boyd

It was a paradox in Belfast terms but it was well-known that Lord Pirrie was a Liberal and a Home Ruler and had connections with the late Sir Winston Churchill and Mr. John Redmond who was a Nationalist M.P. There was an occasion in 1912 when a meeting was arranged in Celtic Park and the three of them had to leave in quite a hurry. But, despite that, Lord Pirrie was looked up to by the shipyard workers and by the people generally.

There was almost a feeling of awe when he walked in procession around the yard, as he did many times. The messenger had to walk so many paces behind with the coats over his shoulder in case the rain came on, Lady Pirrie was with them, too.

He was a man who was respected and they had great faith in his ability to get work for the shipyard. It's well known that he had a connection with the White Star Line and was successful in getting orders for vessels like the 'Titanic' and the 'Olympic' and the 'Britannic'. He could almost say, "Let me build a ship," and they would let him. As a result he was building liners well ahead of anything else that was being produced in the British Isles at the time.

The people didn't seem to mind that Lord Pirrie had those political ideas. One could imagine that the position would be very different today if the chairman was a Home Ruler.

I remember there was a parody on a well-known hymn "There's not a friend like the good Lord Jesus" and the parody went something like this:

> There's not a friend like the good Lord Pirrie,
> Four nought one, four nought one,
> He bought a house in the heart of Surrey,
> Four nought one, four nought one,
> He who knows all about our struggles,
> He'll get us work till the day is done,
> There's not a friend like the good Lord Pirrie,
> Four nought one, four nought one.

I think that the 'four nought one' was the number of the 'Titanic' or the 'Olympic'.

Jimmy Raymond

Lord Pirrie always had the name of being a hard man. They used to tell a story that when he was on his deathbed he called out, "Hand me my sword!"

"Your sword, Lord Pirrie? What do you want your sword for at this time?"

"I want to take another cut at the wages before I go!"

Joe Henry

The boys now go to the canteen and have their-three course lunch. But in our young days we had our tea at ten o'clock. You got a welding rod and bent it into the letter S, your tea can hanging on the bottom, and a tin of slack or french polish below. You put a match to your french polish and inside half an hour you had a can of good hot tea on a winter morning.

Jim Woods

The best man for making tea, you called him Langford Sullivan. Wherever he was, in the shop or out in a frigate, even in a gun turret, Langford could have got his can boiled. No matter what foreman was juking about.

Joe Henry

He used to carry a wee mustard tin with the tea and sugar mixed. It was dropped in and then he made sure that the tea leaves had a good plump so as they turned over on their backs to make sure that the tea was a proper strong brew.

John Gibb

Jim Donaghy

The Mongoose — he was the funniest man I ever met. When Sammy Coates and I were working at the number 15 crane at the water's edge The Mongoose he done the pumps. He had a pot and a pan and he was always cooking.

He made sausages one day and we caught mackerel the next day and they went into the same pan. It was black, pure black. They thought it made good tea. The Mongoose never would have washed it out. So a couple of days went on and we were still catching mackerel. As you know, the fry came up the side of the boat and all we had to do was put a bit of silver paper on the hook and they went for it. They didn't know the difference and we used to get plenty of mackerel. A couple of days after, at the meal hour, Sammy and me had stew.

The Mongoose had stew, too, but he had made his stew in the same pan, you know the mackerel fat. You can imagine the state of the pan. It was serious. Anyway, there was a man worked with us called Jimmy Gibson and he walked up to the hut where The Mongoose was cooking and he says, "Yum, yum". To tell you the truth I was afraid to go near the place, to even smell the cooking, but I says to Jimmy, "What's up, Jimmy?"

"I forgot my piece", he says. "I've a big can of tea but nothing to eat".

Says I, "The Mongoose will not see you starve. Go over and rap the door".

He went over and rapped the door and the Mongoose opened the door and says, "Take your spoon and get stuck into this."

It was the stew warmed up in the old mackerel fat. Poor Gibson said he was never as much embarrassed in his living life. He just had to eat it and say it was lovely. The Mongoose thought it was great stuff. We were sitting over, killing ourselves laughing.

I met him one day in Paddy Lambe's and he called me over and says, "Will you ever forget that day with The Mongoose?"

Herbie Fitzsimmons

There's one story I'll always remember. It happened to me one day in Mr. Rebbeck's time. We were coming one day from the blacksmith's shop, me and my mate, and we had all our gear on a handcart. We were just pushing the handcart through the gate when this big car drew up. It was thirty or forty years ago.

He stopped us, Mr. Rebbeck stopped us. Then he got out of the car and he says, "Where are you going with that?" We told him and he says, "Just wait a wee minute there, lads."

He goes down to the blacksmith's shop and he comes out again with six blacksmiths and six sledge hammers. "Take that drilling gear off that handcart," he says. We took it off, drilling machines and pipes and everything, and he turned round and he says to the blacksmiths, "Smash that handcart up."

So the blacksmiths smashed the handcart to smithereens, wheels and all, and we were standing watching them. Then Mr. Rebbeck turns round and says to us, "Now I have a fleet of lorries here," he says, "we're not having mules down in the shipyard".

So we were pleased enough. He went round and he didn't leave a handcart but what he smashed. So we used to load the gear on the lorries and we sat in the lorry and the lorry took us down to the job. There wasn't a handcart about the place.

The handcarts are back, right enough, but there's no Mr. Rebbeck about the place now.

Harry Lowry

There was an old red leader, a very serious man, and they called him the **Bald Eagle,** and he was spraying the outside of the ship on the waterside. And the staging that he had was a gangway attached to the crane, and the crane naturally lowered him as he went further down the shell. So, it came down very close to the water and the crane man put his feet on the brake to stop, but the gangway still went on down.

The Bald Eagle went with it, right below the water, and evenually the crane man decided the only way to get it stopped was to reverse the engine. So the story goes that **the Bald Eagle** came right out of the water and he was still spraying away at the side of the shell!

Jim Woods

Well, as a matter of fact, I worked alongside Sammy Thompson (the playwright). The first time I ever met Sammy Thompson was up in the town. He worked for a firm I was serving my time with, a firm called C. & J. Graham, of Cliftonpark Avenue. He got this job to do in this Methodist Minister's manse, and I was Sammy's apprentice.

Well, Sammy was a shipyard man out and out, and he didn't know anything about painting in the town — sashes, as we call them, you know the push-up-and-down jobs. You push them out, you paint your meeting rail and you do your races, and I'd to show him how to go about this.

But as a brush hand, he was a superb brush hand, like. In those days you used a lot of enamel and stuff like that and Sammy could have enamelled a door, you could see your face in it. But a very independent chap. I'll tell you how he got the sack.

There was one morning, you started at twenty-five past eight in those days, and Sammy was a wee bit late, and he hadn't been there too long, you know. The boss says to him, "Well, Sam, what kept you?"

"Well," he says, "I just couldn't make it."

"Is that the best excuse you can give me?"

So Sammy says, "It's the only one I'm going to give you." So they parted ways. Sammy got his cards. So that was the last I saw of Sam But I used to love his crack, he was a terrific talker and I used to love listening to his yarns.

Frankie Flynn

Going back a lock of years ago, you were a rich man if you had a good pair of boots on. **Marrow Bone** he had boots all right but he had no soles on the boots. He used to go all round the deck when everybody had knocked off — he had the knack of putting his toes out through the hole in the boot and turning a cigarette packet over to see if anyone had dropped a few cigarettes. There was another two brothers used to work up the road. One was always complaining of pains and the other old fellow he was always moaning and they called one of them **Aches-and-Pains** and the other one **Trouble-and-Strife.** The Martin brothers. One of them actually lived in the morgue at Laganbank. Aye, he lived in the morgue at Laganbank Road. His wife was a caretaker and they lived there.

Well, Joe himself courted old Annie McBride for over fifty years and then she done the dirt on him, she went and died. And they never married. Never married, never married. You would have seen him and her walking up the road — you know Fusco's ice-cream shop there on the Newtownards Road? Well, I used to be up there and you would have seen them on a Saturday night with a big poke going up the Newtownards Road, out courting, out for a bit of a dander.

Alec McAvoy

I remember the launch of the 'Canberra' and there was quite a lot of dignatories down that particular day, Gene Tunney, the boxer, for instance. I think the Queen actually launched the ship and there was this Yank with a big cigar and a ten-gallon hat and with all these cameras strung round him and he had been watching the launch and taking these photographs.

When the launch was over he came over to this wee labourer and he says, "Hi guy, could you tell me where the urinal is?" and the wee labourer turned round and says, "Yea, I think that's her sitting over there with the three funnels on her."

Frankie Flynn

There used to be a wee helper here called Charlie Nailer. He used to work along with a plumber. And the plumber had a whistle and if he was away at the fore end of the boat he blew the whistle and the wee helper run up. But it ended up everybody on the ship got a whistle and they kept blowing it. They had Charlie running all over the place, down the engine room and up, and by the time he got home at night I think he was exhausted.

Jim Woods

Down in this neck of the woods, there's nothing only bad weather, nothing only rain. You can see it coming down over the Knockagh Hill there. And you'd maybe have a bit of deck painted in, and the next thing down comes the rain and the work's ruined. Sometimes you'd get behind in the work.

Now and again we have to go away on trips to get the painting on the ship finished. There's a lot of us has been away all over the place so we call ourselves the Harland Globetrotters.

Joe Henry

On one trip the ship broke down and we were all brought into a wee port called Walrus Bay and we were there for about a week. German West Africa it was then, and after a few days the Germans sent up word to the ship "Would you like to play a football match?"

We had nothing only shipyard boots, steel toecaps and all. We said, "Certainly," so we cut off our overalls at the waist and at the knees and rigged ourselves out as near presentable as we could and out came the Germans. They were immaculate. We started to play anyway, I don't think we crossed the half-way line at all in the first half. They were all over us.

Harry Lowry

At half-time they brought out their cans of beer and whether they got half drunk or not I don't know. But we had a wee bit of a debate that we would change tactics and I changed my position from outside right to referee with the agreement of the Germans. The match started again and there was a lad from Southampton on our crew. He says, "Harry, we are not going to get even across the line." I says, "Look, kick the ball as near as you can to the penalty area."

By this time the Germans were winning about eight-nil. Says I, "Get as near to the box as you can." Sure enough now, the German was about two feet from this guy. I blew the whistle straight away and pointed to the spot and all the Germans were round me like clegs but eventually they took it in good part.

I told him "Now hold it and I will go behind the goals with the camera, and I will take a shot of our boat scoring the goal."

He missed by about four yards!

Solly Lipsitz

Billy Coalbags was one of the characters that I remember very clearly. He used always to smoke a pipe. At that time during the war about every five or six weeks there used to be a sort of a concert party which took place during lunch time, known as 'the meal hour'. There was a makeshift stage placed near the entrance to the Queen's Road. All the acts in this concert party derived from the actual work force itself; they didn't import the acts. I remember, for instance, there was a brass band that used to play popular selections of Victorian and Edwardian music. There was one particular man that used to get up and sing his own monologues. He actually sang this one about **Billy Coalbags** to the tune of "John Brown's Body."

I see we have old Coalbags here at the centre of the floor,
They say that he has smoked a pipe since he was nearly four.
Nobody knows the day or hour the shipyard he did join
But it's said he helped machinemen since King Billy crossed the Boyne.

And that always brought the house down. They were all very fond of **Billy Coalbags.**

Solly Lipsitz.

Solly Lipsitz   Well, there were two men in particular in the Engine Works that I remember. First of all, there was the manager of the whole works, a man called Athol Blair, and then there was the manager of the Queen's Works, Walter Brown. Now Athol Blair wasn't a man that was very often seen around the Queen's Works. But Walter Brown he certainly was, he walked up and down so many times a day.

He was a diminutive little man, a Scotsman, and he used to walk with his head sort of jutted forward — he reminded me somewhat in his walk of Groucho Marx. But it was amazing that, as soon as the grapevine indicated that either of these men was in the vicinity, something strange happened. You can well imagine in a place like the yard there was a lot of big strong men.

Yet somehow or other, when they heard of the arrival of these two men on the premises, their faces tended to go just a little bit paler, and you would see them bent over their benches and over their machines in a way that wasn't usual. It was just that these men exerted such a tremendous personality about them. It really had a tremendous effect on the workforce.

Frankie Flynn

Darkie McQuillan kept everybody going. He had a Tommy Cooper hat and he didn't laugh, he roared, you know, like a football match. Darkie, he used to come in on the morning with a wee bag, you know, a wee shopping bag, and he had a loaf in it, a pound of butter and an egg, a knife and fork, if he had a knife and fork, sometimes it was only a hack saw blade.

Well, at dinner time you would have seen him and he would have went and got an old bit of a board and he threw it down on the ground and the sliced loaf came out and the butter and then he had a wee tin — you know a bean tin, that was his can — and he set that on the fire with the water and then he threw the egg into it and boiled the egg and then he lifted the egg out and put the tea in. He was about seventy-odd when he died and then they tell you all about hygiene and all. It didn't worry him.

Darkie would come in on a Monday morning with a half-decent shirt on, maybe a pink one with a nice collar. Then maybe on Wednesday he would have come in with a blue shirt on, and maybe on Friday a white shirt on. But none of the other shirts in below ever came off. He had seven shirts. That's true. He had seven shirts. One on top of the other. Not only that, he had his sleeping trousers on. He had a pair of trousers on and another pair of trousers on and another pair of trousers on. He lived rather rough, to say the least.

There was some one went to his house one night to visit him and of course Darkie says, "Come on in."

"Och, no I'll not bother, Darkie."

"Come on in, I'll make you a cup of tea."

Of course, the fellow was having none of this — "Naw, I'm just up to give you a message."

He eventually coaxed this particular chap in to his living room and there was Darkie with the fire going and a big lump of stager's plank, one end on the stool and one end on the fire, he just kept pushing it in. He was the best ould fellow for fixing TVs and washing machines, lawnmowers, vacuum cleaners.

But the wife got a new vacuum cleaner and I had an old TV and I asked him one day did he want them both to mess about with and he say, "Oh yes, I'll take them." So that night I got my young lad to throw them in the boot of the motor and I took them over.

You see the house? There was no curtains nor nothing and the light was blaring out and I rang the bell. That's enough. Darkie looks out of the top room — he's in bed — "I'll be down in a minute," — so I went and took them in and he says to me, "I got an apple tart today. Do you want a cup of tea?" The cup and saucer was lying for three weeks. It never seen water but I took the tea. He had a big plank in the fire about eight foot long and he had a chair below the other end.

I said, "Are you not scared of that falling out?" and he said "That will not fall out", and he gave it a big kick into the grate. He kept kicking it in. It was gravity fed before such a thing was introduced. Aye, he was a rough man.

Well, not only that. He used to work here up to eight o'clock at night and I don't know whether you were ever up the Collin Glen Road, away up past Dunmurry. There used to be a tip there. Well, Darkie used to work here until eight o'clock at night and he went home and he got an ould pram out. He went up to the tip and got a load of scrap. The people kicked up about him. The people were getting rid of scrap and he was bringing it back. He was some man Darkie.

Herbie Fitzsimmons and Robert Wade, two drillers.

Chapter Fourteen

Retirement

Herbie Fitzsimmons

Herbie, you're retiring this year. How long have you been here?

I'll be forty-eight years in the shipyard on the 6th June and I never had a black mark against my name.

What trade have you followed?

I'm a driller by trade, it is the only job I ever had and I always liked it.

Do you feel like retiring?

If they'd let me stay on I'd stay on. This is my second home.

You were fond of the work?

I always did plenty of overtime and I put the money by for a rainy day.

How do you think you'll feel when you leave?

I'll be leaving here on the 6th June. I don't know what it'll be like when I have to leave, I won't know until I leave.

Have you any plans for a new life?

I'll feel it odd for I've no hobbies, nor nothing. I'll have to get a wee job outside somewhere. This work here was my whole life.

You might just take it easy.

I could go down to the caravan, I bought a caravan you see, down in Millisle. We could go down there, me and the wife, just kick about and enjoy ourselves.

Epilogue

Solly Lipsitz

The people there, the workforce there, were wonderful. They were a wonderful crowd of people. You could talk about university education — I don't think that there is any university that could ever give you the same sort of experience of life as the people in that shipyard. They are the salt of the earth.

"Steelchest, Nail in the Boot and The Barking Dog" was made by Flying Fox Films for transmission on Channel 4 and RTE

It won the Premier Prize in the Golden Harp International Film Festival in 1986.

Camera	David Barker
assistant	Conor Hammond
Sound	Deke Thompson
	Gerry McCann
Dubbing	Tony McHugh
Editing	Mathilde Blum
assistant	Michael Quinn
Production	Bernie Morrison
team	Catherine Hammond
Commentary	Damian Gorman
Music	John Anderson
Produced and	
Directed by	David Hammond